MAKING SENSE OF METHODS IN THE CLASSROOM

A Pedagogical Presence

Anne Hill

Rowman & Littlefield Education
Lanham, Maryland • Toronto • Oxford
2006

Published in the United States of America
by Rowman & Littlefield Education
A Division of Rowman & Littlefield Publishers, Inc.
A wholly owned subsidiary of The Rowman & Littlefield Publishing Group, Inc.
4501 Forbes Boulevard, Suite 200, Lanham, Maryland 20706
www.rowmaneducation.com

PO Box 317
Oxford
OX2 9RU, UK

British Library Cataloguing in Publication Information Available

Library of Congress Cataloging-in-Publication Data

Hill, Anne, 1949–
    Making sense of methods in the classroom : a pedagogical presence / Anne
Hill.
        p.   cm.
    Includes bibliographical references and index.
    ISBN 1-57886-315-5 (hardcover : alk. paper)—ISBN 1-57886-316-3
(pbk. : alk. paper)
        1. Teaching.   2. Teachers—Attitudes.   3. Teacher-student relationships.
I. Title.
LB1775.H46   2005
371.102—dc22   2005016825

⊗ ™The paper used in this publication meets the minimum requirements of
American National Standard for Information Sciences—Permanence of Paper
for Printed Library Materials, ANSI/NISO Z39.48–1992. Manufactured in the
United States of America.

To Bill, Arden, and David

CONTENTS

ACKNOWLEDGMENTS

The support of family is essential in a task like this. It is also essential to have the support of a professional community. I must thank Jan Blakey, Val Buzzeo, Terry Carson, Jean Clandinin, Karyn Cooper, Lorene Everett-Turner, Madeleine Grumet, Anna Kirova, Stephanie Perrin, Heather Raymond, Mary Linn Sage, Daiyo Sawada, Al Solinski, Lesley Sonnen, Max van Manen, Geoff Wilfong-Pritchard, Darlene Witte, and Grazia Wood.

INTRODUCTION

It would be a challenge to make sense of what goes on in a classroom without being present in one. The title of this book—*Making Sense of Methods in the Classroom: A Pedagogical Presence*—is a deliberate play on words. It is through our senses that we experience being present in the classroom and through our rational thought we can (sometimes) make sense of what goes on in the classroom. We—the author, the teachers, and the children who created the body of this book—invite the reader to explore multiple expressions and meanings that may help make sense of what being a teacher in the classroom means.

Each day my colleagues and I stand at the doorways of schools and classrooms greeting children and parents. We stand at these doorways in our relationships with home and school, between private and public, and within the traditions and diversities of our languages and cultures. We stand between the structures of *technik*—that is, the technical guidelines and legislative mandates of curricular content—and the ambiguity of being, where we sense the humanness of our personal knowledge and pedagogical relationships with the children.

Writing a book about being in classrooms with young children is a challenging task. The forms and the contexts of print differ from the forms and contents of the classrooms where young children and teachers spend so much of their day. The movement, the spontaneity, and the variety of voices in classrooms and schools will not stay still, as print does, for a long, reflective look or for a review of unchanging content. And yet, perhaps, it is this movement between the linear and neatly categorized form of text and the intersubjective flux of relations in our day-to-day life in schools that creates an opportunity for shattering this linear unity and the releasing of alternative possibilities.

It is important to talk about possibilities. With an attitude that acknowledges acceptance of the possible, thought opens to question the meaning of what it is to be pedagogically present with children in their first years in school. What the author, teachers, and children offer in this book are expressions of daily classroom experiences, of what has been said and of what has been understood but remains unsaid. The unsaid is experienced and understood *outside the words*, as one of my colleagues says. However, needing words, we have used them, as we would use a sculpting tool or a paintbrush. The resulting visible expression of pedagogical presence, which takes on the form of text, remains connected within the whole of our human experience, just as music takes form through notes seen and heard, and in the way that music is experienced through our being, between the notes that form the visible on paper and the sound that we perceive outside these notes. Through the sense-making of the embodied form, the experience of the classroom takes on a pattern of meaning.

What we are accustomed to sharing with each other through glances and gestures, staff-room stories, laughter, tears, and silences, we share now through words. It is as if this shared meaning and knowing now ride on the back of these words, as if language were a winged dragon released from the stories we read to the children, powerful with myth and mystery, capable of carrying us from what is known into an unknown territory.

The book tells about our experiences and understandings of being pedagogically present in classrooms with young children. What we have written will be familiar to many readers. The winged-dragon language of poets, philosophers, and storytellers of ancient myths will resonate with the sense of something familiar but as yet unarticulated. It is the hope of those who put together the text of this book that the reader will say "I knew this" and so discover the words through which they can share their knowing.

Researchers in education will recognize the methodologies of qualitative research, specifically hermeneutic and phenomenological inquiry, as well as techniques borrowed from the literature of action research. However, they will discover these methodologies have frequently shifted in form as they have become part of another form—that is, the experience of being in a classroom with young children. Teachers will recognize the shifting of form and the process of adapting techniques. Student teachers beginning to step inside the doorways of classrooms, no longer as the student but with an interest in the pedagogical attitude, will be introduced to the embodied experience of making sense of what they have encountered as they have been instructed in courses on how to teach.

In a search for words to express a shared meaning in the midst of such multiplicities, I am drawn to T. S. Eliot (1961) and his poem *Burnt Norton*. Eliot wrote the poem after walking through a seventeenth-century house named Burnt Norton. Thoughts of times past, present, and future, the flux and fragility of life, prompted him to write that what is "only living can only die" (p. 174). He makes us believe, however, that words can have another presence in time. Words, through the form and pattern of thought and language, have the potential to reach through time, although they too are subject to the flux of the changing world. Words, he says, after they are spoken, "reach into the silence" through form and pattern (p. 174). The pattern remains and reaches into the stillness of an interval in which end and beginning are indistinguishable. "And the end and the beginning were always there" (p. 174). As Eliot walked through the 300-year-old house, he envisioned words as structures, words that "crack and sometimes break, under the burden" and the tension of the structure (p. 175). Words, like other structures will "decay with imprecision, will not stay in place" (p. 175). Eliot suggests that only by the form—the pattern—can words or music reach the stillness, where there will be decay, but never a stillness, only an interval of possibility, a potential, momentarily located "between un-being and being" (p. 175). His verse suggests that the words forming the text of this book will strain and sometimes break under the tension of interpretation, revealing only fragments of understanding. And although the experience of teaching and learning to teach may be somewhat like that of playing a piece of music, even that will decay. Only by the form or pattern will words reach a place of stillness, an interval where thought does not decay.

In a time when tips, tricks, and techniques have become common words in the literature about so much of what we do, talk about words breaking and decaying with imprecision does not inspire confidence. However, I share the beliefs of Parker Palmer—teaching is about creating spaces, about being present and being real in those spaces. We cannot be present and real if we do not recognize the limitations of words.

Awareness of the form or the pattern of words that we use in our pedagogical relationship with children begins with a question that challenges the mindfulness of our presence with the children in our classrooms. Are we present with them? Are we *there*, with a precise and focused attention, watching and listening?

An embodied, organic, questioning attitude becomes, in the words of Madeleine Grumet, "a model of aesthetic form for it establishes the ground for the deliberate shaping of pedagogical experience that is the development of curriculum" (personal communication, 1996). An exploration of the character and meaning of aesthetic form necessitates a return to the original meaning of the word, that is, "an analysis of sensibility" so that we "come nearer to the language and the sense of the ancients" (Kant, as cited in Diffey, 1995, p. 63). The virtue in doing this is that we are thus able to interpret an ancient understanding of reflection, an understanding lost to us because we have for a long time given precedence to the technical-rational and assigned primacy to the visual. In this book the reader will discover how an ancient understanding of reflection may be helpful in enriching our current understanding of the relationship between reflection and developing teaching practices, and how this enables teachers to form and re-form the child's world of the classroom. The power to form and re-form is a paradoxical power, as unbounding as that of the dragons of mythology on whose backs we may fly to shift our perspective, and as limiting as the fire of their wrath-filled territorial claims.

To speak of aesthetic form enables us to speak of a sensibility of perception, of unity, balance, tensions, transformations, movement, and appearances. The word play on the double meaning of "sense" is not lost. The whole of the embodied experience necessarily includes a playful sense of humor, as those who have listened in on children's conversations know well. This sense of play is sustained through the to-and-fro movement within the space between public and private, home and school, *technik* and the ambiguity of being that is essential in an investigation of pedagogical presence. Laughter, and tears too, are part of the whole of the experience. An awareness of the role and the meaning of aesthetic form in our teaching practice enables us to sustain the integrity of the pedagogical relationships between and among child, teacher, and curricular requirements (Cooper & Hill, 2000).

The text of our experience becomes a pattern of words, itself a whole of a kind, even while revealing only fragments of understandings, and even while in the forming it is already "decaying" and "imprecise," as T. S. Eliot says.

Teachers know that in the classroom, words do strain, words do not always stay in place any more than children do, and yet teachers also know there is a routine, a rhythm, and a pattern that comes to be after a time. Perhaps this is just what Eliot means. Perhaps it is this decay and imprecision that allows for possibilities, for new spaces that await the changing fragments and understandings of our day-to-day teaching practice. Perhaps it is this decay and imprecision that enables a re-forming and transforming of our pedagogical relationships with young children. As teachers think about what to do tomorrow and in the next unit, and search programs of studies for the language that codifies our instruction of the day, the pieces need putting together. Perhaps this process is what teachers finally call long-range plans.

As you read you will find that the words of teachers do not stay still. Thoughts and words help one transcend the other in the growth of understanding our teaching practice. This is how we make the dragon-flight into unknown realms of understanding. However, you will find a pattern in the movement, and I believe it is this pattern that sustains the cyclical flux through which we teach. You will find that we are discovering nothing new—only reminders of ancient truths, the truths of myth and of reflection, the truths of Heraclitus' cyclical flux. We experience the flow of being, until we say "Enough. This will be an end for now."

We begin with a re-forming of a question that has been asked of children in classrooms every day for decades. The question is, "Are you present?" In this book, it is teachers who are asking themselves, "Am I present?"

❶

ARE YOU PRESENT?

I have become a question for myself.

—Augustine, as cited in Arendt, 1978, p. 85

A day at school begins with finding out who is "present" and who is "absent." How mundane. Too ordinary, repetitive, and predictable to even think about. And yet, if we listen closely, we hear differences in assumptions about being present. In a kindergarten classroom the teacher asks, "Is John here?" A child who came in with John when the bell rang says, "No." Another child cries out, "Yes, he is!" The first child is adamant. "No, he's not here!" A third child says, "I saw him in the hall." The teacher says, "John is here" and marks John "present." And so the children see that for the teacher, to be "present" means "being anywhere inside the school."

I have never asked myself if I too am present. Perhaps I should. I am here, in the school, and that has always been sufficient reasoning. My colleagues and I are present in the school, like John. Sometimes I would like to be like John, still out in the hall or lingering in the staff room, clinging to the aroma of coffee and the camaraderie of my colleagues. There have been days when I wished I were not present, and days when I have stood at the door of my classroom, looking toward the outer door, hoping that Johnny or Suzie would not be "present" today. Yet there are also days when I want to be there, when I am thrilled to see how the children respond to the chicks that are beginning to hatch, to listen to their responses to the book that I am reading to them, to take part in developing the project that some children had begun the day before.

When I am at school, the sense of "being there" is supported by the embodied sense of all that constitutes life in schools with young children. I hear the click of the clock as the hand jumps to another minute, thus I am attuned to the rhythm of school time and routines. The voices of colleagues run through conversations, so I am aware of intricate connections and tensions, of shifting intensities. There is much we do not speak of, yet we understand. Our language is fragmented. Much is said and much is not. The silence surrounding what is not said becomes as significant as what is perceptible to our senses. Like the paintings by the Canadian artists Janvier and Morriseau, in which lines delineate form, revealing both the seen (animals, person) and the unseen flux of relationship, our words flow in lines that suggest substance, hint at form, and reveal what is not represented.

Outside on the playground, as I talk with a parent, a child may skid by, teetering on a sheet of ice, exclaiming to me, "Mrs. Hill, this is just like melted cheese!" while another comes tearfully complaining that George has pushed him off the tire and George wasn't there first. Standing there, the parent and I hear a child who plays with language, and another who—at that moment in time—finds little language with which to shape his world. Through the whirlwind of a train made of children and hoops, we sense the potential power of this community of children who will re-create the world. Yet for each of us—teacher, parent, and child—the meanings are not identical. The parent might recall visits the cheese skater has made to her home to play with her daughter. She may have never known a child like George and might wonder if perhaps he should be "getting some extra help since he doesn't know how to behave." We are both present in these spaces with the children, although not in the same way.

When the children enter the school, I greet them as their teacher, not as the parent helping me that day might greet them. I must *be there* ready to enter into a pedagogical relationship with the children. As a colleague says, we must be there, "taking time to stand, watching, in the process of constantly trying to understand how to help a child learn."

WHAT TEACHERS SAY

At recess breaks, over morning coffee, and in hallways we share familiar questions with each other. We ask, "How's it going?" and "How's so and so?" and we wait for answers. We want to know what each other is doing, especially if we are teaching the same grade, or if we have the supervision duty following the person we are talking to. We have a need to know if we can get some ideas from our colleague, whether these are ideas about resources, techniques, or what is happening out on the playground.

Like families and villages, schools are communities where it helps to know what everyone else is doing. The many ways in which we all are present—how we are feeling, what we are doing, what we hope and plan to do—all this has an influence on our day.

When I talk with my colleagues and say that I am asking myself these same questions about how things are going, or that I ask myself questions about how I am feeling, and just what it is I am really doing at this moment and how this may be affecting the children, then my colleagues laugh and say to me that this could be a dangerous sign! But when we sit down and talk, and I ask "No, seriously, what is it to be there, to be pedagogically present with the children?" then there is a pause. More often than not, this pause is followed by a response that comes in the form of an anecdote, a story, or a joke. Frequently the jokes are accompanied by a story and are offered as comic relief, in the form of what we named "teacher jokes." For example, there is the joke that goes like this:

Two teachers are talking about the number of years they have been teaching. They say that a colleague has been teaching longer.

"She has 12 years' experience."

"No she hasn't," is the reply. "She has one year of experience repeated 12 times over."

Through laughter, this colleague expressed her sense of understanding and concern about the meaning of pedagogical presence with young children. Another colleague told me of her concern about relationships with children and curriculum, saying,

The thing is, some teachers don't teach children, they teach "Grade 3!" It doesn't matter what some of these kids can do, or that those books aren't even approved any more, they just take them out of the storage room and photocopy them and do the same old stuff. Sarah's determined. She went in the cupboard when George was on leave and threw the stuff out. It hasn't been approved for years! It should have been thrown out years ago!

This teacher expressed her belief that to *be there* in a school meant that the teacher had to *be there* in relation to the learning needs of the child. It wasn't enough to teach a curriculum that was familiar. It was necessary to know what the children were able to do, and to choose resources that would be responsive to their pedagogical needs. It was necessary to be prepared to change every year as the children changed.

Several years ago when I was struggling with how I could respond to the needs of several children in my class who were having trouble with the demands of the curriculum content, I talked to an older, more experienced colleague who said to me, very slowly and with pauses between sentences,

> You have to be there, be all there. That is the crux of it. It's perception. You try to look at the different things that would get in the way. The main thing is to be all there, to be aware of yourself, but also empty. You can't be all tied up. You're just empty, then there's more room to see, to hear, to feel. Then you're more ready.

He looked at me and smiled when he said, "Then you're more ready." I thought then that he must have known I have days when I am not empty, when I am "all tied up" into a solid, impenetrable mass, and I need someone to untie the knots of confusions for me. (Maybe when I am older and more experienced I will know how to do what my older colleague has told me.)

But if I am not there, *all there*, because some part of me is tied up in knots like a congealed and dried-up mass of spaghetti, can I see, or hear, or feel through that mass? I believe the best place to look for the answers to that question is in the lived experience of our own classrooms. We need to be wherever it is that we want to be present. To say anything else would be more absurd in thought than this sounds in writing.

STUDENT TEACHERS AND KNOCK-KNOCK JOKES

Sometimes, becoming "present" is a long and involved process. Sometimes, it is part of what we learn as student teachers. One afternoon, as I sat on the couch in the staff room, restless and complaining within the knotted confusion of how to help a student teacher interact with the children, a colleague offered a story of her experience with another student teacher during the same week.

It's not like thinking there are all these little heads you put stuff into. They know things. Like those knock-knock jokes we did the other day. The student teacher didn't think they were funny, but the kids all laughed at each other's jokes. The student teacher just stood there looking. I said "Knock-knock. Who's there?" And the kids said, "Who?" and I said, "Boo hoo, don't cry." So they all told knock-knock jokes. You know, [laughing] they're not funny, but the kids think they're really funny. We wrote them down. Each child wrote theirs. I did silent *k* before the *n* and apostrophe in "who's" where there's a contraction! I was going to put them up [the writings, on the wall] but I couldn't get the kids to let them out of their little hands! They took them home but I asked them to bring them back so we could put them up. [Pause] The student teacher just stood there. She didn't think it was funny. But she hasn't been in an elementary classroom since she was in elementary school herself. She's only 19, and she doesn't have any younger brothers or sisters.

This teacher means that when we are teachers, we are there—here—present, not simply somewhere in the school building. She expects that student teachers will learn how to *be there*, and that the ways in which they will be there cannot begin in the same way for each person. The student teachers will change as they work with the children.

For this teacher, pedagogical presence is an opening of vision, a widening expanse of perception within which she perceives the children learning. She expects that the student teacher will learn to know the open spaces through which she can learn to extend her field of perception.

Once; when we were student teachers, we too might have stood there, just looking. But now we are teachers and our sense of pedagogical presence is not what it was. There is nothing static; there is no end, no finished point about our sense of pedagogical presence.

YOU DON'T GET IT ONE DAY AND HAVE IT FOREVER

For many teachers the meaning of "presence" does not appear one day and stay with you so that you have it always ever after that. It is not accomplished simply through the act of standing there at a doorway or anywhere else in the school. The student teacher's sense of presence is not my colleague's sense. My colleague acknowledges that the young student teacher in her class is there, present in the only way that she knows, "standing there, just looking." For the student teacher who has not spent much time with young children, we expect that she will change throughout her practice just as we have changed. Perhaps there will come a time when she will feel like laughing in the sharing of knock-knock jokes with six-year-old children. Perhaps then she will see and hear the children's determination to master reading and writing skills and to know the confusion they encounter when sounds and symbol associations do not follow the rule. Perhaps it is this seeing and hearing that will enable the student teacher to know something of what it is to be there in a pedagogical relationship with young children.

My colleague's conversation is helpful as we think about the different ways in which we stand and see the children. Time slips by as we teach year after year and I often forget what it was that I did not know when I began teaching. What I know seems to be so much a part of me that I would compare it to what Polanyi (1958) says of personal knowing: our own knowing is a knowledge that dissolves like sugar into tea—it is present, but not apparent.

The teacher I spoke to about the knotted sense of confusion that I felt in finding ways to help a student teacher reminded me that I must be patient and help the student teacher experience being in this place where we see the smiles and hear the laughter of children at their knock-knock jokes. She reminded me that we, who had many more days being present with children in classrooms, must accept that a student teacher might not laugh at knock-knock jokes, and we must invite her to stay, to listen, and watch.

The challenge of putting together the thinking about how and what to teach, with the experience of making this happen in a pedagogical relation with the children in a classroom, prompts teachers to ask each other, tongue-in-cheek, "Have you got it all together?" Teachers learn to *put it together* and attempt to show student teachers how a lesson in phonics comes together for the children. My colleague's very practical knowledge and embodied wisdom is expressed simply and clearly, with sense and sensibility. She is saying that the student teacher was not going to make sense of children and knock-knock jokes in the curriculum until she experienced the difference between *thinking about* the idea of learning how to teach silent *k* and *experiencing the idea* with her whole body *in relation* to the child's body of laughter.

The simplicity of expression that this teacher offers in her knock-knock anecdote often cloaks a wisdom that is seen to be more elaborate when clothed in the language of academic thought. Take, for example, the following quotation from a conversation that is about the very idea we have just discussed. As you read this, think about the teacher in the knock-knock story as she enables the children to *actualize* the symbolic workings of the *Idea* (a phonetic skill) that has been expressed in the texts of teachers' guides, the scope and sequence charts, and the mandated curriculum. Create in your mind a scene in which the teacher is cast here in the role of subject, produced twice—once as the curriculum (which assumes the role of Idea) and once by the workings of the children's responses.

> The subject, it will be suggested, is unlike signs, [it is] inseparable from differences of intensity: the workings of differences of intensities of the body-subject determine the Ideas' actualization in distinct and differentiated qualities. Put simply: no subject without a body. The subject is therefore produced twice: by the differential and symbolic workings of the Idea—that is its transcendental determination—and by the workings of differences of intensity—its empirical determination. . . . [We experience] a sort of skin of differentiating sense. (Daignault, 1992, pp. 208 209)

Here, one must pick the threads of this elaborate weave in order to unravel the simplicity of thought. The writer is saying that it is the relation (or the "differentiated qualities" of the embodied, sensing person) and the "Idea" that determines what it is we see actualized. How much simpler it was when the teacher said this, telling us that it was necessary to experience the difference between thinking about the idea of learning how to teach silent *k* and experiencing the idea with our whole body in relation to the child's body of laughter. The workings of the relation between children and teacher are organic, sensing, differentiating, and enabling the empirical determination that finds expression in humor and enriched language for child and adult. Because the teacher makes a statement in straightforward, unsophisticated words, does this mean the thought is more unsophisticated than when it is expressed in the language of academic discourse? Who is the wiser—academic, teacher, student teacher, or child? Or could it be that all are wise, and only some are seen to be wise?

During their practicum teaching experiences, student teachers spend a great deal of time watching and listening. In our story the student teacher listened to the laughter of others as she stood watching. Perhaps student teachers also become aware of an absence, as they watch others get the joke and ask themselves, "What's so funny?" Perhaps the sense of difference between the laughter of the children and teacher and the student teacher's absence of laughter is of some help as the student teacher begins to develop her classroom observational skills.

An awareness of difference is sensed through our body as the laughter of the children assaults our ears or prompts our body to laughter. The children's joke may not make me laugh, but the child's laughter contrasting with my absence of laughter is what prompts me to laugh. I don't think the joke is a bit funny, but as I listen and watch, I move into the child's world and I am now present—in a pedagogical sense—because I share with the children a knowledge of what it is to play with language. My experience is not theirs, but I share in their moment of laughter, through my own knowing of the joy and humor that can be found in language *play*. It is thus that we discover how we are becoming aware of our *teacher selves*. We are ourselves, who play with language, and we are the teacher who shares in the child's play with language.

We are not surprised that student teachers ask, "What's so funny?" My colleagues and I assume that student teachers will learn many ways of being with children in pedagogical relations. We have watched this happen before; this is why we take on student teachers. We know that they learn a great deal by being with the children. Our concerns are instead how quickly will they learn, with what support, and with what difficulty. In teaching, no matter how experienced you are, "Difficulties are guaranteed!" as a second-grade teacher told me with a toss of her head and a great laugh. Her gesture suggests that, as she tossed her head, so too we ought to toss off notions of certainty, predictability, and of finally, for all time, *getting it all together*.

"You mean," I asked her, "we never can learn all that we need to know in order to do this job with certainty?"

"I keep hoping," she said, "but I should know better!"

It will always be difficult because I will never know everything. I keep hoping I am learning more, but I should know that I will never know it all.

For as long as we are present in schools, we will continue to have difficulties. This is one certainty in the practice of teaching. We share this knowledge that for as long as we are teaching we will continue to have difficulties. As we struggle with these difficulties we hope that we do not become like those colleagues we have occasionally met during our time in schools who, day after day, look over a child's head, gazing at someone or something else as the child speaks to them, or who say to us as we seek advice on how to respond to a difficult child that, "We know how to kick butt, and that is what we should do." We hope that we will continue to talk about our difficulties, even to complain and rage and cry. This, we say, will at least mean that we will not, as one of my colleagues said, "turn into mushrooms—growing in feces in the dark."

Questioning ourselves, feeling frustrations, laughing with another, sensing humor, knowing that the relation we have with a child one moment or one day will shift and change—these are some of the qualities of our experience of being pedagogically present with children. These qualities of relation define the meaning of presence, even as it is articulated in the *Oxford English Dictionary* (1933). Presence is defined as an adjective, "to be in relation." That is, "to be present" is "to be before, to be at hand . . . an adjective of relation, what is called a 'presence' . . . his outward man must communicate and without fail, something of an indwelling power" (1933, pp. 1300–1301). Presence has an inner quality, a quality of relation, of being near one other, communicated and evident.

QUESTIONING OUR PRESENCE

QUESTIONING THE EVERYDAY, THE ORDINARY

At the beginning of the book, I suggested that perhaps I should have asked myself if I too was present, like the children. Why should this question be asked? Why should teachers be asking about the experience of pedagogical presence, and about the meaning of this experience? What can we learn by questioning ourselves as we work with the children and by asking this particular question? Why? Why? What? We may begin to sound like the young children we spend our time with! Like them, we continue to ask, believing in the virtue of questioning, believing that to question will help us understand the relationships between the children's knowing, our personal and professional knowing, teaching practices, curricular programs of studies, and research.

In the busy-ness of daily school life, there is little time to reflect on these questions, to confirm their validity or to generate a language through which to have conversations regarding these questions. In the day-to-day life of teaching, we find little time to speak of it. Though questions often arise, they are whisked away in the flow of the next movement. However, we sometimes choose to make time to pay attention to our fleeting questions. As my colleague Grace said, standing in the middle of a cluster of desks while the six- and seven-year-old children worked on the floor, on the tables at the edges of the room, and by the counters, "We stand, watching, trying to understand how to help the children learn. How can we do it today? And tomorrow? What resources will we use?"

We must question. It is part of the thinking through of our dilemmas and plans. The question of pedagogical presence is significant because *presence* is paradoxically ordinary and elusive. To question being there in a pedagogical relationship is such an ordinary question that on first glance it may appear not to be worth a second thought. It is a taken-for-granted understanding in schools. Of course we are *there*!

Stephen Smith, in his book *Risk and our Pedagogical Relation to Children* (1998), tells us that "being pedagogically present has to do with *challenging* the child with a mindfulness of how the child encounters the world. It has to do with seeing risk as the child may come to see it" (p. 94). Pedagogical presence, he says, is about our own reflections on our relatedness with the child who is before us. Max van Manen in *The Tone of Teaching* (1986) explores what it means to be present as a teacher when he describes teachers who are able to discuss poems and to poetize life, who talk about responsibility and who live a responsible life, who are aware of educational aims and are able to live a deep sense of hope for each child. In other words, the teacher who *walks the talk* of a thoughtful learner is the teacher who is likely to be pedagogically present with children.

These teachers who have taught us about being teachers begin to make sense of what it means to be pedagogically present. It is a beginning that enables us to better express the character and complexity of our classroom teaching and learning relationships with the children. Talk of playgrounds and living a responsible life is at first glance not the stuff of academic pursuits. It has not been generally acknowledged as having the intellectual status of molecular biology or nuclear physics. It is the very ordinary, everyday talk of people who live with young children—parents' talk, not apparently requiring sophisticated thought or language, just the everyday-ness going to the park with a little kid or teaching a child the alphabet, to read simple material, or to add and subtract. Parents do these things too. Years ago teachers of elementary children did not require the same level of education that was compulsory for high school teachers. The job of teaching young children was considered easy enough that a parent could do it. An adequate level of education to qualify for teaching young children was a year or two of normal school or postsecondary education.

However, it is the very *ordinariness* of the experience that hints at a reason for questioning the significance of our pedagogical presence.

What has not been questioned may be revealing. What appears straight-forward and plainly visible may simply be an illusion. Until we question, until we look for what remains unsaid, we may not know as much as we might otherwise have learned. What is ordinary and taken for granted, what is elusive and ambiguous, invites exploration. Just as explorers have ventured into the oceans that everyone knew were there, and discovered unexpected continents and peoples, it is possible to explore the ordinary experience of teaching in classrooms. It is the language of our teaching and learning that is the concern of this book, and so we look to writers who discuss this aspect of the ordinary. From Wittgenstein (1953) and Habermas (1971), we learn that in the ordinariness of language there remain spaces for "reflexive allusions to what has remained unstated" (Habermas, 1971, p. 168). From them and others like them, we learn to value an exploration of the very ordinary condition of *being there* with children, and we thus generate possibilities for expressing our understanding of teaching practice.

ORDINARY TALK IS NOT ALWAYS STRAIGHTFORWARD

Generally we are used to acting and thinking with an end in mind. We intend some result; our behavior is purposeful. However, we can also be like Alice in *Alice's Adventures in Wonderland*. Classroom teachers who read children's literature can understand Alice's fascination with moving toward what is curiouser and curiouser, not knowing where or if the end exists. Movement such as this in our learning about teaching—movement that is often full of wonder, and often just as strange and unfamiliar as Alice's experiences—is frequently indirect. The purpose may not always be evident, and the logic not always visible. Nevertheless, move we must, because move the children do.

What direction shall our movement take? We must ask ourselves if we choose to set ourselves on a linear path of thinking that is directed toward a closure of meaning. Do we explore as if engaged in a grail quest, a search for the truth, an end to our unknowing? Some say that if we were to search along such a linear path of reasoning we would find, as Sallis (1984) says, that "Meaning *as* [italics added] presence becomes, is reduced to, the meaning *of* [italics added] presence . . . that which delimits presence" (p. 601). In other words, meaning *as* pedagogical presence will be sustained for as long as we remain present, and we may well reduce meaning as we distance ourselves and articulate the experience. To be aware of the reduction, and not to mistake our reduction for the whole of what there is to know, is what we must remember. As Eliot (1961) warned, "words strain, crack and sometimes break, under the burden" (p. 175). The burden here is the burden of Descartes, the dichotomy of mind and body. It is a burden that paradoxically limits (as it articulates a distinction within what is embodied in one being) and frees (as we are aware of the possibility of interplay and the dynamic movement that interplay suggests). Awareness of this burden of reason that has been bequeathed to us will help us appreciate the imprecision of our thought.

Thus we attempt to describe the direction of our search and the forms of our questioning and wondering in the classrooms. Presence is seen to be meaning, and meaning to be presence. This becomes an example of the need to accept not knowing and confusion as virtues! Such a circular-seeming twist of words! But the circle, drawn out in time and space, becomes an ever-reaching, organic, and life-generating spiral, like the model of one of life's basic structures, the DNA molecule.

This exploration in which we choose to engage ourselves reminds me of something I was frequently told as I was learning about teaching young children: it is important for teachers of young children to attend to the learning process, not the product. I was told that I might expect to see a painting that was mud colored, the result of story upon story each painted successively on the paper. The important thing was the telling of the story, not the painting. With a similar attitude to understanding meaning, I interpret Sallis to be saying that presence is an act of meaning, just as the child's act of painting is an action of meaning. The focus is on an *act* of being, as opposed to a product. A search for an end to our questioning, or for closure, means that we risk proceeding in a linear manner, establishing boundaries for meaning, and thus limiting the possibility of experiencing beyond those boundaries.

Sallis (1984) recommends a thinking that releases "the torsion in the question of the meaning of presence and twists it free of metaphysical closure" (p. 601). He suggests that a spiraling, recursive quality of thinking will release the energy of torsion and carry us along in the ever-widening, spiraling, and recursive unity of the hermeneutic circle.

A similar circular, spiraling image is suggested by Gallagher (1992). "The more movement in this circle, the larger the circle grows, embracing the expanding context that throws more and more light upon the parts" (p. 59). With more and more light upon the parts, it might be assumed that we would see more clearly. It is not so much the image of more light on the parts that fascinates me, it is the image of the expanding context that appears significant. Expanding context suggests that we might see more widely, and thus our path might be revealed as something other than linear, and more inclusive of broader contexts.

An example of this idea can be found in Vivian Paley's writing. In *The Kindness of Children* (1999), Paley shows us a way to nurture inclusion of children with special needs. Her directions are simple: Make an appropriate space for children to interact with each other, provide them with meaningful objects and time, then watch and listen carefully for the cues they provide to indicate your role in their interactions. *The Kindness of Children* is not a book of instructions, tips, or techniques on how to integrate children with special needs into so-called regular classrooms. It is a story about presence, and the power of people who are present. Paley believes that stories like these teach us about the possibilities for kindness that exist when we listen to the children. "All the more reason then to listen for the soft breath of friendship and carry our reassuring stories above the din. They are the beacons that help illuminate the moral universe" (p. 129).

She describes Teddy, who joins the class along with a group of severely disabled children. None of the children can walk or sit without help. Teddy has a car equipped with supports that make it possible for him to sit in it and move it. Teddy struggles to express a one-word request. With wrenched torso, twitching shoulders, and flinging arms, he asks for his car. He approaches a child playing at being the cashier in the classroom store.

> Once again, Teddy contorts his small frame in order to speak. "Crispies," he whispers, extending a hand as if it contains money. The Indian child at the toy cash register waits patiently for Teddy's request, watching him closely the entire time. How easily the children do this; even the most

impulsive child is not uncomfortable with awkward mannerisms in others. The boy pretends to take money from Teddy, and in exchange, gives him two little cereal boxes, saying, in a clipped accent, "Here you go, sir. Two for the price of one!" It is a simple transaction, such as might be seen any place where children play, but the joy it brings to Teddy's face fills my eyes with tears. What could I ever do to cause him to gaze at me that way? (Paley, 1999, p. 5)

Teachers who read Paley's stories and reflections on her experiences can see the children in their mind's eye. They can sense the joy and the tears welling up, even though, like Vivian Paley, they are still outside the relationship. What can we do as teachers to create and re-create such meaningful experiences for the children? There is no question about what they are learning.

A teacher who was anticipating the end of her teaching career, who knew that she would no longer even be an outsider to these relationships that children develop, told a story explaining one way that she coped with the anticipated loss of such experiences. In her attempt to hold onto the memories, she kept a piece of a child's spontaneous writing on a large whiteboard that she and the children used in her first-grade class.

One of the children had written on the whiteboard, "I love you Sarah," in the corner of board. The teacher said, "I could so easily have erased them, but I couldn't." The few words, "I love you Sarah," were not dismissed or erased because this teacher wanted to preserve both the quality of the thought and the concreteness of the childish writing that revealed the writer's age.

That scrawled message summed up that whole last year I had with the children. Sarah could not speak or write, but she could, with help, use a word program on our classroom computer to speak and write at least in some way. When Sarah sat with her aide at the computer, on the day it was her group's turn to present their versions of the Little Red Hen, and the computer voice read out loud Sarah's story about the Red Hen who went shopping, the children were utterly silent and still. When Sarah finished pressing the mouse with her hand, the story ended, the children burst into spontaneous applause. I was in awe of them. They were always incredibly supportive of each other in such wise and skilled ways, but this time, it was all of them, all together. (Witte-Townsend & Hill, 2005, in press)

No mandated curriculum or tips on teaching could have told a teacher how to create such social cohesion and spontaneous recognition of accomplishment. It happened because the teacher used sound pedagogical practices: she was aware, she watched, she listened, and she believed in the children's abilities to be aware of and respectful of each other. The teacher was present with the children in a pedagogical relationship.

THE TALK IN OTHER DISCIPLINES

Research on presence, as a professional relationship, is reported in the health science literature, especially research related to the concept of nursing care. This research illustrates a conceptualization of presence as related to the nurse/patient relationship. An understanding of "presence" enables "more being" and "becoming" for the nurse in his or her professional practice (Patterson & Zderad, as cited in Gilje, 1992, p. 63).

> The major defining attribute of *presence* was the ability to psychologically or emotionally *be with* or *attend to* a person, place, or object. . . . The concept *presence* is an intersubjective and introsubjective energy exchange with a person, place, object, thought, feeling, or belief that transforms sensory stimuli, imagination, memory, or intuition into a perceived meaningful experience. (1992, p. 61)

In the nursing literature quoted here, these concepts are grounded through the writings of Heidegger (1982) and Buber (1988). Gilje (1992) says, "As described by Heidegger, *being* can be experienced by sharing one's *presence*. As described by Buber, *being* also can be experienced by being in relationship to and with others" (p. 55). For example, Buber (1988) suggests an understanding of presence that "breaks with subject-object ontology . . . the *encounter*, the *relationship*, the *between*—the call of being, defined as presence or co-presence, itself breaks through as 'the ultimate support of meaning'" (Levinas, as cited in Buber, 1988, p. ix).

In other words, Buber also emphasizes the significance of relation in the creation of meaning. There can be no separation and no isolation if we are to have meaning. Therefore presence, as relation, is critical for making sense of *being* (of being who we are). However, presence alone does not suffice. Presence in classrooms (and elsewhere too) is generally accompanied by language. Language is an inseparable aspect of relation. Derrida (1987) suggests that if we discuss the meaning of presence in the philosophical tradition of deconstruction, "the simple practice of language" makes it possible to take apart our accustomed ways of thinking about what we see, about the ordering of thought about our surroundings, the passage of time, and our relations with others. However, he says that even this so-called simple practice will not suffice in the attempt to re-form thinking (p.151). The practice of language transforming (or deconstructing) a pedagogical relation will not suffice. Language requires the body; the act, the gesture, and the face because language is embodied. Language requires mindfulness, awareness of relation, presence. Teaching language forms to young children requires that we take apart our own conceptions and sense of language to make a space for the child's sense of what constitutes language, and the child's contextual experience of language.

A teacher in a first-grade classroom described how she learned something about this from a child who had given up on learning to read halfway through first grade. Every day he was in the habit of coming into the classroom, putting his head down on his arms, and hiding his eyes. He was no longer willing to interact with the teacher or other children, and after a few weeks of this behavior, his teacher began to take him aside for a while each day to play with letters, words, and stories. During the first few sessions he did not respond at all. Suddenly, his teacher told me, one day, as she talked to him and moved plastic letters around on the table in front of him to show how to change "ran" to "pan" and "pan" to "man," he straightened his body slightly, leaned forward, took a letter in his hand, and moved it across the table. There was a twinkle in his eyes as he asked, "What would happen if we put this letter here?" (Witte-Townsend & Hill, 2005, in press). At that moment, because she could see the light in his eyes, hear the question in his voice, and feel the shift in his body, the teacher knew that expression in print was becoming a meaningful part of this child's language. There is no simple practice of language in the presence of young children.

In our pedagogical relationship with the students, language is a play of differences, and meaning for child and teacher may be found in the spaces between those differences. It is Derrida's (1987) concept of *differánce*, that is, the *play* of differences in the whole of what constitutes language, that enables him to say that the practice of language sustains a play of differences. For as long as the play of differences is sustained, closure remains merely immanent, never immediate: To and fro between child and teacher keeps the learning going. There is never an end. Hopefully, the child who asked what would happen if a letter was moved continued to experience the play of differences, made visible through language, in all of his school experiences.

BEGINNING TO MAKE SENSE

The teachers whose stories make this book have described sensations of frustration over the use of old and meaningless resources, of laughter at the children's knock-knock jokes, and grief over the loss of opportunities to be in the company of compassionate, kind children. All these are characteristics of their pedagogical presence. Teachers make sense of the time they take to provide children with appropriate play materials, companions, time, activities, and encouragement. This sense-making involves more than goal setting and the establishment of specific learner objectives. Although these are essential, there is more to making sense of teaching and learning. It is not that goal setting and the defining of objectives are inessential or even less important. There is no linear hierarchy of importance. To think carefully about pedagogical presence helps make sense of teaching and learning precisely because there is no piece that can be left out. Instead, making sense of teaching requires a reconciliation of parts. Reconciliation of parts requires a shift of thinking that moves away from *ascent* or the linear concept of the *great chain of being*, and toward a concept of a world of time and change that is neither static nor constant, but is dynamic and organic, and can be experienced through our bodily presence in the world.

Berman (1989), for example, explains that the experience of presence "is horizontal rather than vertical, and it has a much greater 'feminine' element in it than does our present consciousness. Vertical structures all have a Grail quest behind them; they are a form of male heroics" (p. 311). The experience of presence is a very ordinary experience, but is "terribly difficult, and where the real work lies" (Berman, 1989, p. 310). According to Berman, even paradigm shifts are not the answer. Rather, we must acknowledge our paradigms as the codes they are, and be aware of the "permanent fragility of meaning" (1989, p. 315). His suggestion that the experience of presence has a greater feminine element does not mean that this is a feminist issue. It is a prompt to look for understanding while keeping in mind an awareness of the structures of predominant thinking. Paradigms provide codes for efficient thinking and shared understandings. They are very useful and provide structure for our thinking. However, we must not become bound up in attention to codes so much so that we fail to attend to other ways of thinking. We might respond to opportunities as St. Exupéry (1943) did, when he said to the little prince, "Don't you see—I am very busy with matters of consequence!" (p. 26). The little prince was very angry with St. Exupéry, accusing him of confusing everything, and said,

> Is it not a matter of consequence to try to understand why the flowers go to so much trouble to grow thorns which are never of any use to them? . . . If some one loves a flower, of which just one single blossom grows in all the millions and millions of stars, it is enough to make him happy just to looks at the stars. He can say to himself: "Somewhere my flower is there. . . ." But if the sheep eats the flower, in one moment all his stars will be darkened. . . . And you think that is not important! (pp. 26–27) . . .

> Here then is a great mystery. For you who also love the little prince, and for me, nothing in the universe can be the same if somewhere, we do not know where, a sheep that we never saw has—yes or no?—eaten a rose. . . . And no grown-up will ever understand that this is a matter of so much importance! (p. 91)

Matters of consequence may be small acts or minor acts of inattention. Children, as the little prince did, will consistently bring our attention to the fragility of meaning as we have constructed it—if we are present.

Hélène Cixous (1991) is another who advises exploration without the support of such codes as our paradigms offer. She says,

> As soon as you let yourself be led beyond codes, your body filled with fear and with joy, the words diverge, you are no longer enclosed in the maps

of social constructions, you no longer walk between walls, meanings flow, the world of railways explodes, the air circulates, desires shatter images, passions are no longer chained to genealogies, life is no longer nailed down to generational time, love is no longer shunted off on the course decided upon by the administration of public alliances. And you are returned to your innocence, your possibilities, the abundance of your intensities. Now listen to what your body hadn't dared let surface. (pp. 50–51)

A teacher who was jolted beyond the codes that Cixous describes, whose body filled with dismay, tells us how images can be shattered, and how the body can provide the impetus to listen to previously accepted and unquestioned structures of thinking. She walked into the school office and unexpectedly saw one of her former students there. She told her story this way.

I walk into the school office. I see Christopher. He is standing in the corner, head hung low, body crumpled against the wall. Time stands still. His eyes meet mine. I did not expect this "look" to sweep in from yesterday on the hands of today. Not three feet away stands our school mission statement. It begins: WE RESPECT THE CHILD. (I am the teacher, caught off guard.)

I am a teacher, and I am as well the child of my own remembering. I am a teacher and I am also the mother of my son. I see Christopher and wonder, "How could it be that this *look* in his face has come here, when yesterday and before that I would not have known or seen it? How has this come to be? What should I do now? How can I think about this? I feel for him as I would for my son." (Hill & Cooper, 1995)

The teacher is caught off guard. A body filled with shock and confusion questions images and codes that represent social constructions of behavior and thinking. The sign no longer makes sense.

I understand these writers to claim what Levin (1988) does when he suggests that the sense of presence may not be understood independently from the context it inhabits. It is no longer sufficient to look left and right or up and down as we might in a linear conceptualization of the dialectical or the sequential. Rather, it is possible that our field of perception may open onto horizons in front of, behind, over, and under us simultaneously, even while we are remembering some aspect of this experience but from another context, or being reminded of what we thought we had forgotten!

Thus, it is necessary to acknowledge that the articulation of our experiences of pedagogical presence may be diverse and may be expressed through codes unfamiliar to some. Presence is "not at all a sense defined in terms of traditional substantiality and field independence" (Levin, 1988, p. 244) and we might not proceed in a straightforward, linear fashion.

Even the transformation of this multidimensional experience from action, gesture, glance, and spoken word may take on qualities that are not straightforward. Researchers engaged in paradigms that are coded in a linear mode might record the path of exploration in a manner consistent with that paradigm. However, if the lived experience of pedagogical presence is horizontal, relational, and requires an undoing of conceptual orderings, then we may find the writing of such research to be consistent with this manner of thinking. Just think about what it is to listen to a young child's story or to a child's rage, or to understand children's questions. How do we write about the child who cannot sit at his desk because he will not move out of the corner where he is huddled sobbing—choking out the words that tell you he is worried his mother might be dead by this afternoon? How do we think about the child who forgets a word he sees in print 20 times each day, a word he writes and says and reads in the morning and by late afternoon has forgotten it? How do we understand this child? Is it sufficient to say, "Well he's an Opportunity Kid, you know." Does this help us to know how to plan for the child, how to encourage him to keep working toward reading, how to ease his rage, or to ease the tension in his voice as he responds to another child?

How do we think and how do we write? I am often disappointed that we have become practiced at thinking and writing in codes taken from other disciplines without sufficient thought. I am left with an image, a marketplace of text, in which we exchange a code for money, as we exhibit our expertise in coining a phrase for literal coin.

But if we are to *be there*, to understand, and to respond in ways that enable the child to continue thinking, to question further, then we often must listen and watch in such a way that we hear and see more than language can convey. If we are to be there with the child to challenge,

to risk with the child, to support this venture of learning, then sometimes we have to know something of what was before, and what was
associated with the before. It is not enough to simply learn something
about the children's experiences, we must also learn something of the
experience of others in the child's world, even of our own. The direction
of our understanding is linear and also recursive; one experience is entwined with and within another experience.

3

A RECONCILIATION OF
THEORY AND PRACTICE

Forgive me if I inquire: Just according to whose plan?

—Leonard Cohen, 1993

To investigate the paradigms and codes associated with methodologies of qualitative research is helpful and necessary—and yet, our many years of experience as classroom teachers have left us cautious about techniques and capital-R research. Trends have come and gone. Schools and teachers have seen open area classrooms, phonics workbooks and basal readers, whole language, new math and manipulatives, vision statements, values-based and inquiry-based social studies, no windows in schools, and skylights and trees in schools. Forgive us if we are skeptical. Leonard Cohen says what we are trying to say. My colleagues throw back their heads and laugh when they read Cohen's (1993) song "The Story of Isaac" in the political and economic context of their teaching. They listen in utter silence when I play the tape of children's playground voices followed by Cohen's earthy voice as he sings his interpretation of Isaac's experience on the mountain with Abraham. "You who build these altars now," you who stand now with "hatchets," above the gods and demons, cannot know what it is to be at the mercy of someone who is entranced with the power of words (p. 140). As Isaac, Cohen says, "A scheme is not a vision" (p. 140) and he asks forgiveness for questioning "Just according to whose plan?" before he will agree to anything.

As I read Cohen's poem, and the question repeats in my mind, I am reminded of a song the children at school sometimes sing. (The children's voices sometimes quite literally ring in my ears even after they have gone home.) They sing, "This is the song that never ends. Someone started singing it not knowing what it was—because, this is the song that never ends." And their song repeats itself to me, unbidden. Once begun, it will not leave my thoughts. I hear over and over, "A scheme is not a vision" and "You who build these altars now. . . . Forgive me if I inquire, just according to whose plan?" Whose plan, these altars?

How are we to question and understand what it is to be pedagogically present with the children? A scheme will not suffice. A scheme is not a vision. A scheme, or *schema* in the tradition of educational research, is

> usually thought of as an abstract event structure or a knowledge pattern with slots that can be filled in by particular agents, objects and other contextual specifics. But this is too abstract and intellectualized, for it leaves out the way these structures are realized in, and can subtly transform, our embodied experiences. The cycle of a typical school day is felt in our bodies; it is lived out as the phenomenological pacing and patterning of our activities. (Johnson, 1989, p. 370)

Words, when bound in schema, lack a dynamic, organic quality. It is the poet who most often forms words into something other than schema. Poets, who paradoxically have a reputation for entrancing, for creating the magical quality of words through the beauty of the word, have also a reputation for employing the pen as a weapon, mightier than the sword. Caputo (1987) captures the thought in a few words. Writing is, he says, "a stylus, a stiletto, used to unseat the metaphysical and apocalyptic horsemen" (p. 152).

The poet Cohen and the philosopher Caputo, and others as well (Lovejoy, 1936/1964; Taylor, 1987, 1991), suggest we must be aware that the altars we create with our language and that we name "scientific paradigms" are not artifices on which we educators may sacrifice our children. They suggest to me that I must hesitate, reflect, shift my range of vision, and be willing to question my beliefs and motives. The children and their repetitive song remind me that once a pattern of thought is established, it is very easy to continue without knowing either source or end.

BEGINNING TO SEE AS A TEACHER

When former kindergarten teacher Margaret Olson (1989) talks about novice and experienced teachers creating environments for learning, she suggests that "As one begins to dwell as a teacher, to be a teacher on the inside, one also begins to see as a teacher, and thus is more able to build, design a room for learning" (p. 175). One is also more able to "see the students in and through their reality. Only then is it possible to reach out to the needs of the students and make one's presence felt throughout the room" (p. 181). Ted Aoki (1993) suggests that we shift away from distanced sociological, anthropological, and technological understandings of our lived teaching experiences. He suggests that we consider instead what he speaks of as *indwelling*, which is a word also used by Michael Polanyi, in his book *Personal Knowledge* (1958). Aoki (1993) tells us that the lived experience in teacher-children relations is

> a pedagogical situation within which teachers and students experience life. For when a teacher begins to indwell with students, the environment ceases to be environment, and in its place comes into being a lived pedagogical situation pregnantly alive with possibilities in the presence of people. (p. 112)

To indwell, as Aoki describes it, suggests that meaning and understanding associated with experience are supported through relationship. One lives within a space of relations with an-other, who also occupies that space and moment. As we dwell in our homes and workplaces, we live in relation to the way our spaces are divided—kitchen, living room, office, elevators, doors. We also live in relation to other people in these spaces and times.

I remember that when I began teaching I was often frustrated by the children's behavior as they entered large, undefined spaces such as gymnasiums. I felt I was losing control of the children when they entered a gym or other large indoor play space. Inevitably they wanted to leap and run, to stretch out their arms, to reach up and out. All around them was space into which they attempted to move.

As I reflect on these moments, the scenes play back as if I were reviewing the scene through some amateur's attempt at video recording, creating scattered, jerky, and interrupted scenes. I wonder now how the children experienced these scenes. I wonder if for the children there was no separation of the ontological sense of the environment and the epistemological knowing of space. In my life I make these distinctions; perhaps the children do not.

For example, I recently helped a friend make decisions about where to place her furniture in a newly rented apartment. Both our young children came along. My friend and I had come supplied with measuring tapes and paper. We moved from room to room, recording dimensions. In halls we stepped over the children as they rolled along with their knees tucked up. In living and dining rooms, we moved aside as the children swooped like bats with arms outstretched through these larger spaces. My friend and I planned to come to know about the environment of the apartment through the linear measures of meters. The children, however, measured the space with their bodies to determine the relation of their bodies to the space. Certainly our purposes were different. My friend and I needed to know where furniture would fit, and the children needed to know how they would fit. We laughed at ourselves as we watched our children. How different we were, and yet, how much the same.

For my friend and for me, our knowing is the cultural background of a linear measure, of representation and social convention regarding the use of living space. Our knowing is also the recollection of childhood play, our own rolling and twirling in spaces now distant. We are the grown-up children of our parents. We are mothers and teachers too, and thus our knowing is also an awareness of children learning. A pedagogical interest entwines with the interest of parent and remembered child.

In many places, I am learning from children how to *indwell* in the spaces we share. As the children jumped and rolled, their arms and legs stretching and sometimes flailing in the larger spaces, children and space existed in relation with each other, one dwelling within the other. The children came to know these spaces in relation to their bodies and their movements. This was the structure of their knowing, formed as they explored their lived space. Through the children's interaction within the gym and the apartment, their environment became meaningful space, as Aoki suggested it would for teachers who begin to indwell with students in pedagogical relations. Polanyi (1958) would say that

The arts of doing and knowing, the valuation and the understanding of meanings, are thus seen to be only different aspects of the act of extending our person into the subsidiary awareness of particulars which compose a whole. . . . It is the act of commitment in its full structure that saves personal knowledge from being merely subjective. . . . It is an act of hope. (p. 65)

The children and my friend and I had different ways of doing, in order to know. We created meaning through dwelling in the spaces. The knowledge gained was not merely subjective, it was comprised of many parts—perhaps not all possible parts, but more than one. In each case, there was a commitment to find meaning in the knowledge. Whether we are parents, teachers, or children, to indwell is to experience what is external to our body through our body. It is thus through our body that we are able to attend to the world in which we live, that is, our cultural, physical experience. The structure of such knowing is a structure of to-and-fro movement through the situated body, and it is this to-and-fro relational movement that sustains knowing. "The fact that exteriorization kills meaning confirms the sense-giving powers of indwelling" (Polanyi, 1958, p. 185). As my friend and I acknowledged the language of the children, we became aware of the way in which the children were establishing a sense of the space in the apartment. For the children's purposes, our measurements, being exterior to their bodies, had no meaning. The children made sense of the space from the inside out.

In the gym and the apartment, our sense-making of space was an experience of relation that supported meaning as we moved within and between forms of knowing, our own and the children's. Our laughter signaled a knowing, unarticulated before reflection and conversation. This unarticulated knowing is a tacit knowing, personal, and without public form. Yet our presence with children, our dwelling with them, enables us to recognize the relationships in our coming to make sense of our experiences.

The identification of tacit knowing with indwelling involves a shift of emphasis in our conception of tacit knowing. We had envisaged tacit knowing in the first place as a way to know more than we can tell. . . . Since we were not attending to the particulars in themselves, we could not identify them: but if we now regard the integration of particulars as an interiorization, it takes on a more positive character. It now becomes a means of making certain things function as the proximal terms of knowing, so that instead of observing them in themselves, we may be aware of them in their bearing on the comprehensive entity which they constitute. It brings home to us that it is not by looking at things, but by dwelling in them, that we understand their joint meaning. (Polanyi, 1966/1983, pp. 17–18)

We indwell when environment ceases to be environment and becomes instead an experience of possibilities. There is no line of subject-object separation here, but rather a recursive spiral of encounter and re-encounter that is similar to the energy of torsion expressed by Sallis (1984). We circle around our past experiences and the children's present rolling and twirlings. Beginnings and endings of experiences, our own and the children's, are difficult to separate, though each is distinguishable. Past and present intertwine, each sustaining the experience, so that my friend and I walk around the children—we do not stop the encounter of child with environment. We laugh with the joy of our own memories and the satisfaction of seeing our children find ways to explore their relations with living/living space. We are, as Pinar (1988) says, able to "attune [ourselves] to a situation" (p. 143).

The indwelling of our teaching practice "gestures toward a path of engagement rather than the mere reflex of academic comparisons" (Buber, 1988, p. ix). The path of engagement is suggested by Aoki, Buber, and Polanyi as an understanding of living in relation, *through* our bodies, *in* the world. It is by dwelling in this relational structure that we are able to understand meaning. To be pedagogically present with young children is to follow this gesture toward a path of engagement.

I believe it is important to add Stephen Smith's (1991) reminder of a connection between a sense of pedagogical presence and a sense of security. He suggests that a sense of pedagogical presence is a sense of presence that lets being come forth and that this requires the bringing of a sense of security to the pedagogical atmosphere so that being may come forth. "Being present pedagogically thus requires that we fully *encounter* the riskiness of the child's activity" (p. 450). The child risks in the act of being pedagogically present. It may be that the teacher does as well.

This is the path of our departure as we attempt to understand and articulate the meaning and significance of pedagogical presence with young children—risky, necessarily straying from a linear presentation, involving past, present, and expectations of the future. It is a path of engagement situated in a relational flux of differences. The writing that records this path must follow its lead and decipher meaning with the help of appropriate codes.

MAKING SENSE OF THE CLASSROOM: BEYOND THE CODES OF METHODOLOGIES AND CURRICULA

To be there, to be pedagogically present, must begin with being there. This is so simple a statement that it sounds ridiculous in the writing and no doubt also in the reading. But wait, listen for a moment for the possibilities that lie beneath the obvious. One of the first things I learned when I began teaching was to stop and count to 10, to watch and listen while I counted. It was one of the most valuable strategies I ever learned. I invite you to practice it here, watching and listening to this story.

Be Curious: You Might Discover Something

Jennifer and four other girls were going back and forth, back and forth, between the writing center and the storybook center carrying papers. They had already carried all the playhouse pots and spoons to the storybook center. I began to feel like commanding a loud and firm "Stop!"—but I have learned just enough to know that I sometimes really do not know what is going on. I walked over to check. Jennifer seemed to be directing others. There was an audience of three children seated in chairs placed across the entrance to the story center. I asked Jennifer what she was doing. "It's Jingle Bells," she said. "Yes, I could tell that, but what is this all about?" I was puzzled and the noise from the pots and spoons was beginning to bother me. She looked at me directly and firmly said, "It's the death of harmony." She showed me her music—five wiggly lines with notes. The others had sheets of music too. I asked Jennifer if she knew what harmony meant, since I knew she did not take music lessons although her brother did. I had read music to the children, showing them the symbols I was using, as I have read all sorts of signs and symbols to them. Jennifer responded, "Harmony is when all the music goes together and it sounds nice."

To myself I said, "Right!" And I thought they were just making a noise with a bunch of pots! The death of harmony! It is more than that now. The child who told me her creation was *The Death of Harmony* reminds me, as Derrida (1987) does too, that meaning is "not a matter of immediate presence or self-presence . . . underlying it is always the differentiated structure of a language that goes beyond anything present, a system of contrasts and differences that are not themselves present" (p. 121). Here is an opportunity to engage in language that offers a to and fro of what is of immediate presence and what is not. The children, the pots and pans, the tune of Jingle Bells, print, and language too are present. For me what was not present was an awareness of *The Death of Harmony*. Meaning became clear when this difference was shown to me. The to and fro of language, the contrasts that were not present to me, were an opportunistic moment in which both the child and teacher were able to acknowledge that our presence is a sharing of language, a sharing of the subtle differences of meaning in language.

Again, in another classroom, a first-grade class, again within the children's world, I find another way to make sense of pedagogical presence. I began to read the story *I'll Meet You at the Cucumbers* (Moore, 1989) to the class seated in a semicircle at my feet. In this story, Adam the mouse has been invited to go on a journey to the city with his friend Junius. Junius has made the trip often, but Adam is alternately terrified and fascinated. As they cross a bridge, Adam looks down and sees the clouds reflected in the river. He cries out to his friend that he sees a "sky mirror" (p. 24). As Adam sees it, the sky gives light to the river. His friend looks again to see what Adam sees, and says, "You do make a fellow look twice, Adam" (p. 24–25). Adam and Junius offer us an opportunity to learn about risk when embarking on a journey into the unknown. To be with children and be reminded to look twice, and thus to discover an opportunity to learn something unexpected and full of wonder, to be with children and be invited to listen—these are opportunities to establish an interaction, a relationship. Without interaction, we cannot participate in a dialogue; without dialogue, it is difficult to form and re-form the language of our teaching practice.

Smith (1991) suggests that we should listen to the voice of children, and that while we are engaged in research of an interpretive, hermeneutic character, we should listen not to speculate on the *right* answer or to try out one's methodological framework or instructional strategy, but to the interplay of part and whole. Listening in this way is consistent with the ethics of a hermeneutic research process, an ethics that affirms and preserves the integrity of the teaching-learning situation even while we engage in enquiry (Smith, 1991). It is an ethic that acknowledges the local and ambiguous character of the teaching-learning experience (Gallagher, 1992). It is an ethic in which the interplay of part and whole generates a flux of movement.

Listen to the Children: Anna's Letter

One fall afternoon, on a visit to Helen's kindergarten/first-grade classroom, I sat down at the children's writing table—for no reason other than it was the nearest place to sit and I felt like sitting. Two girls sat at the writing table, each with paper and pencil in hand. The papers were intended to become letters to "Dear Frog." The children in the class had heard many *Frog and Toad* stories during the week. Their teacher said they could write letters to Frog or Toad during their "choice" time. Frog or Toad would answer their letters. I sat, listening and watching. One of the girls, Anna, could be heard softly singing. I leaned forward and moved closer to hear the words. I listened to the shift of tones and the repetitive rhythm of her short song. In her soft, clear voice, Anna was composing the letter that she has allowed me to share.[1] She sang the words over and over as she began to write. Then she stopped singing. Her voice became focused on the sounds of letters. I listened to the sounds of words being split up and put together. From voice to shape, I saw the text begin to assume form. Anna's friend offered help with the spelling of some words when Anna stopped and looked at her. Anna asked me how to spell *world*.

> Dear Frog,
>   Where do you live? I want to know if you can come to school and see the world?
>   Come to my birthday.

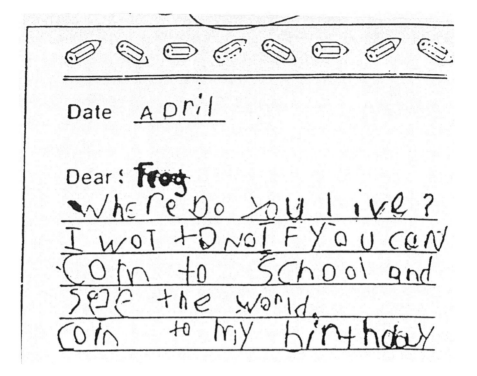

Date A pril

Dear : Frog
Where Do you live?
I wot to nol f you can
com to school and
see the world.
com   to my birthday

Anna's teacher walked by; I looked up at her with eyebrows raised, caught her eye, and pointed at Anna's paper. She grinned, a glowing kind of smile, and almost floated on air as she moved on her way. Neither of us wanted to interrupt this moment with words. It was too precious to change in any way.

Now, when I pick up and reread Anna's letter to Frog, I hold what seems to be the tracing of an outline for the casts of our meaning and our writing. *Trace* seems to be an appropriate word to use. In an early childhood classroom, I use the word *trace* so often that it comes readily to me. I often outline a word or letter and encourage a child to trace it. Needing to re-create the experience of being with the children in a textual form or a public language, I search for outlines around which I might trace. Here in my experience with Anna is an outline around which I may form words through which to share understandings.

The outline begins with an invitation. In the actions surrounding the creation of this letter are the tracings of an invitation to share a relationship, to "see the world." To accept an invitation requires that I move from one space to another, a coming-from and going-to, and that I move in relation to some other. It is around the other that I move, their form shaping my moves, and my moves shaping their form, and so on and so on in a recursive, cyclical pattern.

As I hold Anna's writing, I recall listening to her voice sound out the text, watching the shape of text begin to form. In a shift of form, from language sung, sounding voice, and printed text, Anna's writing is a tracing of the movement of these differences. Holding Anna's letter, I trace this movement of differences, a shift of the sound and sense of that experience with the children writing letters to Frog, as well as recollections of other times and places. More than a sequence of events, or a demonstrated sequence of skills, I hold an outline of the elusive relation of movement between song and sound, text and meaning, school and world, past and present.

Like other pieces of children's work that I save, Anna's letter acts to remind me of watching children learn to write, creating text out of sound and shape. I hang these up around my computer. There are a few photographs, a tattered bookmark, some drawings, a magic wand, and a small, smooth stone. These too are traces, like Anna's letter. Around each I can trace the shape of a moment, a relationship, a whole series of relationships and moments. I can go over and over them, like a child tracing a letter or a word. I can retrace the experience again and again, through the colors in the picture, by recalling the box of crayons, the bits of grubby crayon paper lying in the bottom of the plastic container, or the smell of wax in the warmth of sunlight. Memories of what it was to be present in those places with the children are re-created. These recollections of crayon paper and broken crayons evoke memories of my own crayon boxes when I was a child. Drawings evoke memories of the long-haired princesses I used to draw as a child. I can hear the rattle of felt pens in plastic bins being rifled through in rapid search for *the* red, in haste before a classmate chooses that color. I can hear the slow sound of pencil lead on paper as Anna forms her letters. Around the fragments of one moment held in my hand, I can trace the web of time through now and then, here and there—from this moment, now, right here as I write, back to *there* of my own childhood.

Anna's meaning was formed in song as she sang the words she intended to write and as she sang the parts that she split into phonemic parts. Hélène Cixous (1991) in her book *Coming to Writing and Other Essays* wrote, "Soundsense, singsound, bloodsong, everything's already written, all the meanings are cast" (p. 58). How much alike these two writers are, one just beginning, and one well established. Soundsense and singsound was Anna's bloodsong too, the body of her voice. So too the meaning for a teacher's encounter with the question of pedagogical presence can become formed through the bodies and voices of the children and the teachers. It is only necessary to transform and re-form the meaning that is cast in a language form consisting of blood and body—an eyebrow raised, a glow, the intermingled tones of song and voice, of children's swinging feet, and toppling blocks.

Meaning and sense-making undergo deconstruction. We have seen educational fads and trends come and go and come again, and we have come to understand what Caputo (1987) means when he writes about knowing a truth. He offers the idea of "Nietzsche's (1969) woman-truth, the woman who is not fooled by herself, whose own truth is to know there is no truth, not even the truth of the woman" (p. 151). We have learned to do what is as close to the *truth* or to the *right thing* as is possible for us in our day-to-day relations with children, but this does not mean that what we are doing is *the* truth or *the* right thing. We are only making attempts. For example, one day as I fretted about finding words to explain what I was thinking, and how to describe the idea of pedagogical presence, my colleague Grace told me, "Don't worry about the words. Never mind. Just leave it for a few weeks and we'll just keep doing what we're doing [which was working together in the classroom with me sitting down to jot notes and later having conversations to try to understand what it was we had been doing]. We'll find words for it later." And we do find words. We find them, of course, where we so often do—within our relations with the children, often unexpectedly, surprisingly.

This is what Kristeva (1981) means when she talks about the writing of language, referring to Derrida's words *"des traces de differánces"* (p. 23). Kristeva writes about Derrida's belief that language suggests more than a *structured system* of differences. She explains that Derrida goes beyond understanding language as a system of normative attributes. Language is a flux of relational movement in which difference indicates the traces of relations within language. As we saw with Anna's song, writing, and her intention to communicate meaning, language is a movement traced by the relation of sound and symbol with sense—a multidimensional movement of relational structures that frees interpretation from arbitrary or single, linear realities of one dimension. Kristeva claims it is in this way that one of the generative forms of language we call reading and writing becomes visible within the play of system/movement or structure/flux.

The point made by Kristeva and Derrida is that language and writing (as an aspect of language) are not linear systems. They are intimate aspects of our humanity, as interrelational and generative as our physical bodies. Arendt (1978) too reminds us that language is generative and interrelational when she suggests (reminding us that Aristotle said the same thing), that language enables

> analogies, metaphors, and emblems [that] are the threads by which the mind holds on to the world even when, absent-mindedly, it has lost direct contact with it, and they guarantee the unity of human experience. . . . They serve as models to give us our bearings lest we stagger blindly among experiences that our bodily senses with their relative certainty of knowledge cannot guide us through. (p. 109)

Anna's invitation to see the world is a metaphor, which, like a thread, connects me with the world of the classroom when I risk losing direct contact with it. Like the larger world, this world of the classroom is

> made of words, thoughts, and objects not given to us by nature, or the gods, but created by men to serve their humanity. . . . And so the world . . . is both a gift and a work. It is what limits and frees. It is what shelters, what frames our acts. (Ricard, 1994, p. 48)

The child's classroom world is both a gift that I may appreciate and a work that I may value. The classroom both limits and sets free; it shelters and frames thought and action.

IMMERSE YOURSELF IN THE LANGUAGE
OF SCHOOLS

Lived experience in schools, this phenomenon of living in relation with colleagues, children, and curricula, this living with(in), or indwelling, enables us to discover the language through which we begin to understand. I write and rewrite the teachers' stories and my own, searching for just the words, just the expression, just so. The stories become more than words on paper, they are more than can be meant by describing them as narratives or anecdotes. As we engage in this phenomenological writing and rewriting, relationships among our classroom language, our stories, memories, anecdotes, and narrative develops. I discover, as I look back through some of my old journal notes, that I had written to myself that

> Narrative can drop dead on the paper if we simply repeat the teachers' stories in[to] [sic] the now. Writing teachers' narratives is a question of doing, of being. Recovery, recollection, and repetition are not the same as a reduction to *the meaning of*.

How is this dilemma resolved by other writers? Rilke was told by Rodin to go and sit at the zoo and watch the animals until he had something to write. (I suppose a sculptor would say that.) Rilke did what he was told. He wrote *The Panther* and other poems from his intense, prolonged observations. We are told by Deleuze (1993) to consider looking at the writing of James Joyce. "Joyce's words, accurately described as having 'multiple roots,' shattered the linear unity of the word, even of language, only to posit a cyclic unity of the sentences, text, or knowledge" (p. 28). Another writer who makes suggestions to help me undo the knots of confusion about writing to make sense of what the children write and say is Lyotard. In *The Postmodern Condition: A Report of Knowledge*, Lyotard (1984) said that the

> work of Proust and that of Joyce both allude to something which does not allow itself to be made present. . . . [A postmodern dilemma which makes it necessary and possible to search] for new presentations, not in order to employ them but in order to impart a stronger sense of the unpresentable. (pp. 80–81)

What a relief to find eminent writers saying this! What seems unpresentable and unsuitable for linear form may become presentable after all. After the teachers and I have engaged in writing and rewriting, perhaps finally, in Joyce's writing we may find a model for a narrative form that reveals traces of relation. The form of Joyce's writing leads the reader in a spiraling, multidimensional form of thought. I imagine a spiraling presentation that might look like something I drew while chatting with a colleague during a lull in parent interviews. The first-grade teacher and I were trying to find ways to articulate to some well-educated and highly involved parents what it was we were doing with their children and why. I drew a line that spiraled out from a center point that indicated the beginning of something the first-grade teacher had been teaching the children in science. The spiraling line was my attempt to describe the circularity, connectedness, and direction of our instructional strategies. There was a purpose and a relationship, an integration of the multitude of things we did in each part of the day with the children. The challenge remained: How could we convey our purposes and strategies to parents who were accustomed to well-defined clarity of thought? At least my colleague and I knew that we had to convey the many connections we were making for the children in all subject areas.

APPRECIATE THE MANY FORMS OF NARRATIVES

Anecdotes, stories, and jokes are some of the forms that narratives take as teachers share with each other the understandings of the meaning of pedagogical presence. They are what Charles Taylor (1991) refers to as the subtle "languages of personal resonances," a way to talk about connecting and linking beyond the self (p. 90). Narratives may even at times be subversive, especially when tensions are felt, and when teachers feel a need to empower themselves. For example, when a student teacher expressed concern about being able to cover the curriculum with the second-grade class, the supervising teacher, with a straight face, gave her instructions: First, take the children's books from their desks, then have the children sit on their books. "Now," she said, "You have covered the curriculum." This was more than play with words. In this story of a story, although there is humor and perhaps some sarcasm, it is still possible to see what Clandinin and Connelly (1991) meant when they said that a "teacher's story shapes the curricular experience of the learner, the ways in which theory and practice interrelate, the relationship between teaching and political ideology, and the politics of curriculum research" (1991, p. 387). In this case, the student teacher learned something of the possible ways in which theory and practice might be interrelated, even subverted.

Teachers interpret language and text from an understanding of being in the world with parents, children, colleagues, and political ideologies. Teachers' narratives have the potential to reveal an understanding that is inseparable from their being in the world, from their being in schoolrooms with young children. The narratives are one way that teachers create and re-create their own lifelong, teacher-education programs. The understandings acquired are more than a grasp of facts. Facts regarding techniques that contribute to instructional strategies, curriculum content, instructional objectives, children's home environments, children's skills and needs—these facts teachers know. However, "Understanding is not concerned with grasping a fact but with apprehending a possibility of being" (Ricoeur, 1991, p. 66), and teachers are aware of the possibilities for children's learning and of their own process of becoming a teacher.

LISTEN TO CLASSROOM NARRATIVES

Ceaselessly, humankind has told and retold stories. As a personal and a cultural experience, the telling of stories is a model of our individual and collective *becoming*. Our stories are, as Mark Johnson (1989) says,

> a bodily reality—it [narrative] concerns the very structure of our perceptions, feelings, experiences, and actions. It includes our sense of time and our awareness of the patterning and flow of our experiences. It is what we live through and experience prior to any reflective "telling" of the story in words. (p. 374)

Because classroom narratives are embodied, they are personal. The language resonates with voice, with experiences over time, and with context. In schools, our conversations often proceed in a circular fashion. There is no need to think this is a vicious circle. Rather, we circle back upon the already done and the already said, and the written and rewritten, reforming our thoughts and images. The text of this book emerges through glance and gesture. Like the storytellers of old, my colleagues weave words with hands and eyes, with cadence and pause, through seconds and minutes, now quickly running sentences together in excitement, now slowly. This becomes our experience of narrative as we begin to question together. Remaining connected to the life of the classroom is one way to avoid becoming immersed in an epistemology that, as Charles Taylor (1987) says, is as unconnected with life as a corpse.

It is this relation of movement, a to and fro, a play of system/movement or structure/flux, that enables the generation of text surrounding the question of presence. In the to and fro of child and teacher, child and child, sound-sense becomes language, and language shifts form as text emerges. Such shift of form is familiar to me. After having read aloud fairy tales about frogs and princesses, the imagery of shifting form is so familiar that I cannot hear of a frog without also thinking about the process and possibility of transformation, of person or thought. Being with young children, and being surprised by young children, transforms my teaching practice (Hill, 1994).

BE THOUGHTFUL AND ATTENTIVE

When I sat in Helen's class and watched as Anna began to write her letter to Frog, I was slowly learning a way to tell about what it is to be pedagogically present with a young child learning to write. My words assumed form as Anna's text assumed its form. The sound of voice, and the sense of meaning; these shifted in the to and fro of movement, creating differences and enabling the tracing that makes this visible.

In a similar way, we enter into other pedagogical relationships. We engage in an ethics of continuing relation, of listening with care and attention to the meaningful sounding-out, the relationship of sound and sense, of text and meaning, where thought holds sense. In the child's space, there is that "play" that is the "Dance . . . that bodily felt quality of inwrought thoughtfulness" (Levin, 1985, p. 296). We search for a relationship of sound and sense, of text and meaning. I recall asking a kindergarten child if he understood the story presented through a read-ers' theater presentation done by a ninth-grade class. The vocabulary had been complex, the teenage voices intense, their faces sometimes frightening with expression, their bodies filling the space of our small classroom carpet. I was concerned in case the experience had been overwhelming, so I asked the children what they thought about the per-formance and the story. A child replied, "I didn't know lots of the words but I understood the story." He understood, despite not grasping some of the facts.

In our relationships with children, watching and listening with care and attention, we are thoughtful. It is through this quality of thoughtful-ness, a felt sense of confusion sometimes, of surprise, of wonderment, and of hesitation at other times, that we experience a quality of relation, a to-and-fro movement from one to the other. As we listen, watch, and question, we are likely to discover, as St. Exupery (1943) tells us in his book *The Little Prince*, that we can learn a great deal from children. For example, his little prince met a railway switchman and they talked about the brilliantly lighted express trains that thundered past.

"Are they pursuing the first travelers?" demanded the little prince.

"They are pursuing nothing at all," said the switchman. "They are asleep in there, or if they are not asleep they are yawning. Only the chil-dren are flattening their noses against the window-panes."

"Only the children know what they are looking for," said the little prince. (p. 73)

Only the children know. St. Exupery helps me to remember this. Always the children are part of the greater whole of the experience of teaching, the pedagogic reason for our scholarship, and thus they ought to be part of the effort to learn to teach.

If we are to understand the meaning and significance of pedagogical presence, it is helpful to be attentive to the voices of children. Like D. Smith (1991), I believe that "the voice of the young, the meaning and the place of children in our lives is the most important consideration to be taken up in education today" (p. 188). Listening to children is not only an ethic of a phenomenological-hermeneutic questioning process, it is an ethic that affirms and preserves the integrity of the teaching-learning situation at all times (D. Smith, 1991). If we are to receive the message that Hermes carries to us on winged feet, we surely ought to be listening and watching as well.

Through the movements of their bodies, the expressions on their faces, and the tone in their voices, the children may reveal to us what we have been unable to know (Lippitz, 1986). One of my colleagues says that it is through eavesdropping on the children's conversations that "I know what will work for them. It teaches me how to teach them." I have never read of eavesdropping as an ethic of the hermeneutic process, or of lifelong learning in the classroom! What my colleague means is that children engage in personal conversation in her kindergarten/first-grade classroom. She recognizes this and feels like an intruder; however, she listens because the children's conversations help her to teach the children. She explained through a story. She worked with a small group of children who had difficulties with reading and classroom behaviors. Each day 11 children came to her for an hour. She wanted to move them from the small books they had into beginning chapter books. One day at noon, the teacher saw one of the girls in the library looking at an Amelia Bedelia book, although the girl could not read them on her own. The child said to a friend, "I like these Amelia Bedelia books." My colleague collected enough books so that each child was able to choose a title. A week after the children began working through and reading the Amelia Bedelia books, one of the children, a child who had previously thrown several chapter books across the floor in frustration, wrote in her journal, "I like Amelia BeDelia so so so much," followed by a small heart.

Realizing that the girls in the group enjoyed reading Amelia Bedelia books reminded the teacher that her youngest son, who had difficulty reading when he was in elementary school, still had many copies of *Nate the Great* books, and amazingly, one of the reading series available in the school had a *Nate the Great* story in it as well. She added *Nate the Great* to the novel study, as well as a stuffed dog and an old leather trench coat from the 1970s. Dramatization, her own and the children's, was a great motivator and illustrator of meaning (Witte, Sawada, & Hill, 1997).

It was through eavesdropping that the teacher gathered significant information to help her plan. Through eavesdropping, she also acquired a lizard and several nonfiction books on lizards and snakes, as well as several copies of *The Paper Bag Princess*—but that's another story!

HOW TO MAKE SENSE OF TELLING AND RETELLING STORIES

Listening to children has cautioned me to approach my own altars of meaning and sense-making in the classroom with caution. Children teach us to be cautious of our assumptions, just as Bateson (1979), Caputo (1987), and Lovejoy (1936/1964) advocate caution and willingness to reflect on the unexpected when writing about epistemological assumptions. For example, Lovejoy criticizes "thought-obscuring terms, which one sometimes wished to see expunged from the vocabulary" (p. 6), and "implicit or incompletely explicit assumptions, or more or less unconscious mental habits, operating in the thought of an individual or a generation" (p. 7). Like Taylor (1987, 1991), who concerns himself with images of epistemological corpses, and "iron-caged" bodies of knowledge, Lovejoy states that

> A formulated doctrine is sometimes a relatively inert thing. The conclusion reached by a process of thought is also not infrequently the conclusion of the process of thought. The more significant factor in the matter may be, not the dogmas which certain persons proclaim . . . but the motives or reasons which have led them to it. (Lovejoy, 1936/1964, p. 5)

I do not want to use thought-obscuring terms. My mother once referred to a Ph.D. as being a short term for "piled higher and deeper!" And I do not want to be in the company of Taylor's epistemological corpses. Yet, how do I show that the thoughts and actions of teachers—and often of children, too—demonstrate as much wisdom as many philosophers and poets? How do I enhance the credibility of this thinking that emerges from the classroom?

Since text takes precedence in the form of this presentation, and since the form of language both shapes and contains the *matter* of our text, I have had to ask myself what procedure, what writing style, will preserve the "force under the form" (Derrida, as cited in Rosen, 1986,

p. 227). "Retelling requires imagination and wisdom," Rosen says with reference to Derrida (p. 227). Is there a way to move on from the question that will also be a move away from the instrumental and atomistic understandings, a move that will leave knowledge still connected with life, a way that will be a form of "envisagement, a means of developing perception in keeping with conception" (Langer, 1957, p. 149)? Is there a way to move on from the question of "Am I present?" in a way that will preserve the integrity of teachers' knowledge and expression?

I must continue to question. It is necessary to concern myself with integrity in order to choose the way up Isaac's mountain carefully. It would be easy to fall back upon unconscious mental habits, but I might risk sacrificing our children on an altar of methodology and thinking. I must remain attentive to the relationship between language, experience, and interpretation. As Eisner (1992) says, "Language is constitutive of experience; it is not simply descriptive, and the way in which the world is parsed has significant value consequences for matters of educational practice" (p. 303). A "spontaneous word may contain a whole becoming" (Merleau-Ponty, 1968, p. 236).

> Just as it is necessary to restore the vertical visible world, so also there is a vertical view of the mind, according to which it is not made up of a multitude of memories, images, judgements, it is one sole movement that one can coin out in judgements, in memories, but that holds them in one sole cluster as a spontaneous word contains a whole becoming, as one sole grasp of the hand contains a whole chunk of space. (Merleau-Ponty, 1968, p. 236)

I watched in wonder one day in the school library as a child in my kindergarten class suddenly clutched his book to himself and called out. With a great gasp, and in one spontaneous motion, he whirled himself up and out of a chair, to stand in front of me, his arms tightly wrapped around the book. "Mrs. Hill! I can read!" His words rang out in a pure tone of joy. Everyone looked. His tiny body seemed at once to throw itself to the world and envelop the book. I experienced the image of a text-enveloping body, the sound of a clear declaration to the world. In this moment and space, language was constitutive in a dynamic, generative, embodied sense. I witnessed a whole becoming, contained and revealed through the embodied language of the child.

The steps taken beyond questioning about pedagogical presence may be like this, quiet moments of routine, shattered suddenly by clusters of *being* that contain a whole becoming. Thus the reader cannot expect to find here a single, linear dimension tracing sense-making of pedagogical presence to a definitive conclusion. It may be, as Merleau-Ponty (1968) describes, a path envisaged as a continuous line, a line that winds and twists, even twisting back upon itself, thus connecting many of its points simultaneously. Like the expressionist painters whose points of color together convey an image of the play of light—an image of movement possible only when points are connected—so too our words touch each other such that one spontaneous word may contain a whole becoming. So too may our experiences in the classrooms with young children wind one upon the other, touching past and future, holding in one movement all that we are or were or may be. The relation between thought, language, and experience, which develops throughout this process, may be constitutive in an organic, generative sense of becoming.

Such a path with language, on the way to knowing, follows ancient pedagogical traditions. For example, Berman (1989) writes about his maternal grandfather's experience in the cheder using honey to write *aleph* and *beys* on his slate, then eating the honey/words, an experience which "evokes an older, poetic use of language which is especially characteristic of Hebrew: the power of the Word" (Berman, 1981, p. 267). "Real knowledge is not merely discursive or literal; it is also, if not first and foremost, sensuous. In fact, it is very nearly erotic, derived from bodily participation in the learning act" (Berman, 1981, p. 269). Such a path toward knowing can also be found in other traditions and cultures. For example, the Chinese ideograph for knowledge includes the concept of heart (Hodgkin, 1985). Thus, I plan to start up the mountain with an understanding of the relation between ontological understanding and the epistemology that I will create with the teachers and the children in their classrooms.

THE VIRTUE OF HESITATION: THOUGHTFUL LISTENING AT THE STILL POINT

Repetition, hesitation, and struggle along the way must be encouraged and expected. Repetition is opportunity for remembering, for reminding, for persuading. I remember being puzzled when a friend complained about the repetition in Rita MacNeil's (1988) song "Working Man," in which she repeats over and over, the phrase, "And I never again will go down." The repetition made sense to me. Would it not make sense to everyone who had repeated a self-made promise to themselves in order to strengthen their resolve? When I am trying to convince myself that I will or will not do something, I talk to myself and say over and over again what it is I will or will not do. Had my friend never repeated his words for a similar purpose?

Hesitation allows opportunity for reflection, for the shifting of our range of vision and a questioning of what we see. Hesitate, as we tell the children, "Look before you cross" and "Look both ways." Being with children in the classroom for more than 25 years has cautioned me to approach *altars* of meaning and sense-making with caution, to look many ways before stepping, and even as the children do, to look back to see the others of my group. We who stand in doorways must look at least in every direction. We pause and question in the classroom with the children as we shift the plan of the curriculum guide so we may respond to the children in the moment and place. The integrity of our questioning demands that we ask, "Whose plan, which path do we use?" It is necessary to ask. Unless we ask who made the path that we see from the doorway, and where it is intended to lead us, we will proceed blindly. We who teach children in schools have already followed multitudes of innovative, new curriculum designs, building designs, and teaching strategies. I am not suggesting we as teachers ought to be resistant to change, only that we think before we take a step. Such a hesitating, questioning stance at the doorway is a daily experience. Each day, as the children come in and out of the schools and classrooms, we wonder if we have made the best decisions for them that day. Have we chosen activities that will help them develop ideas? Will the story hold their interest; pique their curiosity? Will George be able to follow through on this fine motor task? Will Adrianna be as volatile today as she was yesterday? Our questions are of both the curriculum guides and the children.

Our struggle is to continue to search for ways to answer these questions, knowing there is no end. Teachers are accustomed to hesitating as we struggle with thought emerging, forming and reforming. Whose plan will work in this moment, in this place, for these children? And now, whose plan will work to help us move beyond this hesitation in the face of the question of presence?

It might seem that this conversation with myself around the question of pedagogical presence has the character of "the almost [*presque*]" (Barthes, 1985, p. 3). Language is *almost* formed, but not quite visible. Not yet able to say what I want or mean, I pause, as I always have in the classroom before making decisions. This quiet hesitation must not be mistaken for a halt in the effort or for indecision.

THE RETURN TO THE CLASSROOM

I return to the teachers and the children—again. Answers must lie there. Observing again, I watched as a first-grade teacher and the children sat on the carpet, engaged in watching the pattern of movement of leaves and seeds as they fell. On her desk she had the science curriculum guide. This teacher told me that she liked to review the parts of the section on trees that she had highlighted a year or two ago. It helps her pick and choose her way through the curriculum guide. On the carpet with the children, she initiated observations and comments about the leaf that she dropped. Then she looked at several children and asked one to describe what he saw. She watched and listened to this child, responded to him, then asked another. She continued—watching, listening, and responding until she was able to return the children's own comments to them, now connected with each other and transformed to reveal, through language, the intricate precision of a falling leaf. She told me that as she watches she is able to know "what's interesting to the kids. How they're touched by what we do."

Only the beginning of her teaching plan was the same as the plan of the curriculum guide. The rest was created through a process of watching and listening to the children, questioning herself, and responding. She had moved in an ever-expanding spiral of watching and responding, carrying the children's pieces of conversation with her, shifting her original plan in order to respond to the children. As we talked about this process, I drew a spiraling diagram, which at the time seemed to offer a way for us to remember and to talk about the process of changing plans.

Our conversation created the path of the diagram as we circled back on parts of the conversation, returning to the point that was the teacher, and shifting to the children, reaching out into their language. Now the diagram remains as a tracing of the movement that created it. This is the spiraling pattern of our conversation and of the lesson. On each return, there is a point to which we return, not in the same time or course—that point has passed—but up just a bit on the diagram, indicating a movement in time yet a connection to a point already passed. This moment of crossing, this intersection of a three-dimensional model that has pretensions of including the dimension of time, creates a split second of recognition, a brief pause—"Oh yes, I recognize this, but it is different now." It is a moment of stillness—brief, for sure, but there it is, a split second.

It is a good thing to pause in this interlude of time/space. We watch, listen, and question. With the spiral image in my head, and a visual image of the line marking a return, yet not a return to the same point, I like to think about something that T. S. Eliot (1961) said about the turning world and time. There is a "still point," he says, where there is neither movement nor stopping, not a fixed position (p. 172). It is where the "dance" is, "where past and future are gathered" (p. 172) Now I have some words with which to transform my experience. Perhaps Eliot's language form and patterns will help us to keep this moment from slipping, sliding, and perishing under the burden of meaning and our inadequate language abilities. Perhaps, with Eliot's word forms, we could talk again about other moments when we watch and we are able to know, as my colleague said, "What's interesting to the kids. How they're touched by what we do."

How difficult it is to place in time, in sequence, the events of the lesson on the leaf. How difficult it would be to plan and to write a plan for this interaction of teacher, leaf, curriculum, and children. The teacher hesitates, listens. She and I must see the children's faces as they look out at us from behind the images we have made of them. Their eyes hint at what we cannot see or hear or touch. But—at the edges of those images we have made—there a laugh, a giggle, a twinkling eye, or a bit of silence sticks out, and we must pause as they move into our field of vision. Just as Junius realized that the sky is the giver of light to the river, I realize the children too are like the sky. They give light enough for me to see beyond, behind, and around the edges of that image template I have made of them. Leonard Cohen's words repeat themselves, "A scheme is not a vision," and I see that I cannot frame all that goes on around me, because to do so would restrict my vision. When I attempt to create a scheme into which I think I could make sense of what is going on, bits stick out, like the children's faces as they look at me, peering from behind the picture we had made of them, hinting at what cannot be seen or heard or touched. I must turn again to see what lies behind the template I had made. It may only take a second glance, a shift in my chair, a step closer. I have time for that.

In that move/moment is the return to the still point of the turning world, where past and future are gathered, as the teacher makes a decision about her next move in the to and fro of the dance. Thus the interplay of parts became the steps we carved as we made our way up Isaac's mountain. We believed our trek up the mountain was for the purpose of enlightenment, not sacrifice. Enlightenment is not the same as finding the answer. I would not want to leave the reader with the impression that this was all such serious business that the teacher and I believed we were going to find *the* answer once we got the to the top. We have been teaching long enough to stop clinging to the naive belief that there are answers. After all, when the bear went over the mountain, all that he could see was the other side of the mountain!

REPETITION AND PLAY

My colleagues and I have found that as we attempt to make sense of pedagogical presence in our daily practice, dialogue and communication are at times very difficult; however, it is through our continued and persistent interactions that we are able to develop understandings that we share.

> And so here is the answer to the question that I posed at the beginning of this discussion, about the distinction between a confined, institutionalized reason and the free play of reason. It is not a question of choosing be-

tween these alternatives. . . . And so it is a question of vigilance about that and, hence, of exercising a certain double agency, a critique exercised from within, of assuming the role of a treacherous and wily Hermes who subverts, who does an "inside job" on the institution . . . to keep reason in play and to keep the play in reason. (Caputo, 1987, p. 235)

Together we too seek to do an inside job on our practice. We look for an engagement with the interplay of part and whole, where we can play like the child at peek-a-boo, and experience the thrill of throwing on and off the cover of institutional reason to rediscover vision. We resist the somber image of draping altars of reason with "institutional authority" (Caputo, 1987, p. 234) and would rather find reason in the play, and keep the play in reason.

In schools we are very careful about the use of the word *play*. Play is a word that is encumbered with meanings. Everyone thinks they know just what it means, and everyone has his or her own context for this understanding. I have found that the ancient meaning, the traditional meaning, is most helpful for my own understanding of the relationship between play and learning. A very long time ago, in the time of kings and queens, a king decided that his people needed a few days in the year away from their work, time for *spiel*, which meant dance in his language. Thus the people were allowed time for dance. Spiel now means play. Dance has become play. Dance was movement in relation to music, a to and fro of body/music in rhythmic relation. Play, in many disciplines, holds onto this meaning, a to and fro of relation, a relation that generates desired movement.

> Modern research has conceived of play so widely that it is led more or less to the verge of the attitude that is based on subjectivity. . . . If we examine how the word "play" is used and concentrate on its so-called transferred meanings we find talk of the play of light, the play of waves, the play of the component in the bearing-case, the inter-play of limbs, the play of forces, the play of gnats, even a play on words. In each case what is intended is the to-and-fro movement which is not tied to any goal which would bring it to an end. This accords with the original meaning of the word spiel as "dance." (Gadamer, 1984, p. 93)

Understanding this as play, we can encourage an interplay of words, of methodologies, of movement, and of meaning in the relation of teacher and child(ren). Where such play is permitted, we can move to and fro between the words of the child and the teacher, and the words of "institutionalized reason" (Caputo, 1987, p. 235). In the movement of this play, there is no draping of "reason with institutional authority" p. 234), there is, rather, an engagement with the to and fro, the interplay of part and whole, where we play with reason and keep the *reason* in play.

The integrity of the pedagogical relationship, which is an exercise in hermeneutic understanding, demands that we participate in this continuing interaction, a recursive process of movement that I refer to as play. When talking about hermeneutic understanding, Habermas (1971) suggests that interactive participation is critical. "Hermeneutic understanding ties the interpreter to the role of a partner in dialogue. *Only this model of participation in communication learned in interaction* can explain the specific achievement of hermeneutics" (p. 180).

Our professional competence and situational understanding form an insider knowledge that develops through "direct experience which gets stored in memory, not as sets of propositions but as a repertoire of case narratives" (Elliott, 1991, p. 130). His words are strangely like Emerson's of more than a hundred years ago when he said,

> Action is with the scholar subordinate, but it is essential. Without it he is not yet man. Without it thought can never ripen into truth. . . . The preamble of thought, the transition through which it passes from the unconscious to the conscious, is action. Only so much do I know, as I have lived. Instantly we know whose words are loaded with life, and whose are not. . . .
>
> The new deed is yet a part of life,—remains for a time immersed in our unconscious life. In some contemplative hour it detaches itself from life like a ripe fruit, to become a thought of the mind. Instantly it is raised, transfigured. . . . In its grub state, it cannot fly, it cannot shine, it is a dull grub. But suddenly, without observation, the selfsame thing unfurls beautiful wings, and is an angel of wisdom. So is there no fact, no event, in our private history, which shall not, sooner or later, lose its adhesive, inert form, and astonish us by soaring from our body into the empyrean. (Emerson, 1946/1981, p. 59–60)

Emerson may not have struggled to make his grub state of thought take flight. I do not know if the transformation was as easy as he makes it sound. However, I do know that I and many other teachers continue to struggle with this transformation.

AN INSIDE JOB AT PLAY

Through the questioning of pedagogical presence, I have continued to experience opportunity for laughter, for the sharing of teacher jokes that help us to articulate what reason sometimes finds tragic. Those colleagues, whom I also call my friends, cannot completely change the teacher who will not look a child in the eye when the child speaks to him or her, or who photocopies materials that are no longer on the approved list of resources provided to school boards. We persist in working together to change what we can, and when possible, relieve the frustration with humor. An awareness of, and a regard for, these conditions is a reminder of what van Manen (1988) cautions is the danger of living "a half-life, unresponsive to pedagogy, when our scholarly activities are cut off from the pedagogic reason for this scholarship" (p. 441).

Thus it is that reaching an understanding of one moment's lived experience, or what one might call phenomenological closure, becomes part of a recursive cycle of closing and opening. Closure is only that moment between the question and the next awakening. Closure is only an interval in the to-and-fro "play" of system/movement, structure/flux. Paradoxically, although language enables closure, language also "allows for presence in absence by constituting a realm of significance within which the human subject can play" (Grange, 1989, p. 163). And thus we carry what we thought we finished, only to find that it is a key to another arena in which we may play.

As we interact in classrooms with young children, it feels as though we make a conscious effort to *store*, to reflect, to recall, to talk about. We select and reject, as situations change. Sometimes our knowledge remains in what Polanyi (1958) describes as the "ineffable domain" (p. 87) of tacit knowing, where articulation is almost impossible, or is revealed as an "ineptitude of speech, owing to which articulation encumbers the tacit work of thought, [or a case of] symbolic operations that outrun our understanding and thus anticipate novel modes of thought" (p. 86).

As I talk with my colleagues in schools, we struggle to articulate our experiences of the day. We often know that we do not quite know what we are talking about. However, if we were ever to stop simply because our language was inadequate, then we would never know! Just as we tell the children, "You have to try it. You can do this part and I will help you with another part," we assume similar expectations for ourselves. The search for any symbolic aspect of language that will assist us enables us to come closer to knowing. An anecdote, an example, a child's piece of work, a comparison—these all are part of the river, are part of our conversations as thoughts scatter and coalesce, swirling around the boulders, scattered over wide expanses of the rock-strewn river bottom. We are carried by a force, of which we are only one part.

Our daily practice is the ordinary language of life in schools. It is a language perhaps, to use Emerson's words, in a *grub state*, awaiting metamorphosis, or so we might hope, to become a butterfly! It lies entwined within conception (experience) and text, at the "confluence" of biology (gut) and epistemology (Polanyi, 1958, p. 95). There in the space of this confluence, through the language of glance and gesture, telling and retelling, we change the form of our knowledge (often not without a struggle) from tacit to articulate. There are times when "All we can do is gaze in wonderment at the diversity of discursive species, just as we do at the diversity of plant or animal species" (Lyotard, 1984, p. 80). "Duh! Of course that is all we can do!" we could say, as we hear the children say in situations that remind us of this moment of unarticulated amazed confusion or wonderment at the situation. The paradox of language creating both boundaries and horizons is described by Taylor (1991) as "inescapable" and helpful when we want to establish a "background of intelligibility" (p. 37). It is at least a background on which to begin to create a form for the knowing that is in a grub state, awaiting transformation into a form that is intelligible to others.

PURE THEORY: A USED-CAR LOT OF USEFUL PARTS

Time and conversation enable our knowing to emerge in articulate form. For example, as I was ready to leave the school one day, a colleague said that she was "really interested to see what you say about circle times with the children. I don't have much time to think about these ideas in the classroom." She began to talk about spontaneity and teaching young children, and drew me into her wonderings. I lingered in the doorway, as we both began to wonder about spontaneity and circle time. Together we questioned and searched for words through a dialogue about circle time, gathering children together, and spontaneity—all in the same moment of conversation. It did not matter that we do not know right then. The bits of our unknowing stuck out all over, falling in pieces within our conversation, visible in the *umms* and the pauses, the laughter and the unfinished thought! I made notes later about this conversation, so as to keep the thoughts visible. Taking these notes and writing something coherent from the pieces is similar to the moments I spend in the class after the children leave, gathering up the odd pieces of pattern blocks and cubes, and the cutting scraps, the unidentified painting, the fragments of paper with children's sometimes undecipherable but very meaningful writing. As I gather these pieces, I reflect on the day. It reminds me of the act of picking up at home after our youngest son has gone to bed. For each of us participating in the research, the writing is a gathering together of our days, a picking up of thoughts. Later, when we get together to *see* the text that I have created, we question and reflect, entwining these thoughts with those of the new day. Each piece of the writing I did as I watched my colleagues and even myself in my class, and each piece of writing I did as we talked, had scribbled notes added beside it, arrows drawn, diagrams made, and comments added. We teachers have lots to say!

In its research form, the management of this text became problematic. How could we ever turn our understanding of pedagogical presence into words if I did not find some form of writing that would incorporate every piece of thinking? It was in the literature of action research that I found helpful suggestions, even though some of the language of the tradition was unacceptable to me and to the teachers. For example, I described to two of my colleagues something of the suggestions from the literature of action research regarding the management of text. One of the suggestions was that a notebook could be called an "analytic field notebook" (Altrichter, Posch, & Somekh, 1993, p. 91). This was responded to with laughter. "Ha! As if!" The opinion was that our thoughts recorded were anything but analytical and certainly didn't belong in anything with an officious, militaristic title.

But here was an example of what Habermas (1971) was intending when he said that the task of hermeneutics is to bring together the general and individual so that one is part of the other, to value interaction in a dialogue of partnership so that a common understanding is reached. Through thinking about, talking about and writing about, our lived experiences of the classroom (otherwise called our phenomenological hermeneutic methodology), we brought together the language of our experiences (the theoretical and the practical) so that we were able to reach some common understandings. The suggestions found in Altrichter et al. (1993), although not expressed in a language that we thought appropriate, nevertheless enabled the hermeneutic circle of interpretation to be traced through texts in a way that was readily visible.

Habermas (1971) had more to say about the process of hermeneutic inquiry as he continued the idea. It is appropriate to include this here since it also illustrates the perceived difference between the languages of theory and practice. He says there is an

> ontological illusion of pure theory behind which knowledge-constitutive interests become invisible . . . [and this] promotes the fiction that Socratic dialogue is possible everywhere and at any time. . . . It is pure theory, wanting to derive everything from itself, that succumbs to unacknowledged external conditions and becomes ideological. (p. 180)

With an "As if!" the pure theory of the analytical memo succumbs to daily life. The pure theory of analytical memos is dashed to pieces and excluded from the teachers' dialogue. However, as often happens when something is broken, the pieces are picked up. The whole is not something that we could use—however, the pieces are useful. During the research for this text, we picked up a few of these and adapted them to our own situation. It reminded me of an old Cadillac my great-grandfather had in the farmyard under the trees by the fence. We were always afraid to go into it—there were always bees and mice in places like that—but we used to walk around it, whispering in the shade about where it may have been before and where people might have gone in it, that is, when it had parts. My great-grandfather bought it at the beginning of the Second World War. He never drove it, just kept it for parts. The neighbors came to it for parts too. My great-grandfather knew that the whole car would be of no use, gas-guzzler and luxury that it was, but for parts it was a gold mine of opportunity throughout the entire war. And so we too found the action research methodology to be a gold mine of parts. We kept a notebook, but our *memos* were not coded with letters and neatly written into the side margins allowed on each page. We needed an entire facing page for our notes that frequently were diagrams and occasionally photocopies of some small part of a curriculum resource we used or thought we might use.

One of my colleagues suggested I should use different-colored ink for different teachers and for comments, so that we could retrace our thoughts more quickly and easily. (She was always really organized!) So, like explorers who journey to and from the uncharted, we recorded the journey out and the journey back! (I wonder, did explorers' maps look as scribbled up as ours did at times?) We were reluctant to leave a thought un-noted, or not discussed. Sometimes one of the teachers worried about "going off the topic," but still wanted to discuss something of importance at the moment, and so she did. After teaching for many years, we have come to know that it is wise to look carefully at the fragments of thought, both our own and the children's. We have become familiar with thinking about the fragments of children's learning, those fragments that stick out of templates like cuttings from children's tracings, like shavings from their play-dough creations that scatter the floor beneath the desks and tables. Is this fragment the whole head of a gingerbread man template, or a nicked foot? I have come to know that I can learn about children from watching the kinds of errors they make, from watching what they don't pay attention to, and from trying to understand what frustrates them. Our teaching is also a process of eliminating possibilities regarding a child's source of difficulties.

We have had long practice with looking at what does not fit. We are accustomed to a knowing (both our own knowing and children's) that is not flattened under the template of a methodology. When we get stuck and cannot find the words we want in a situation, when we cannot find the words to answer our own questions, my friend and colleague Grace says to me, "Ask me in few months" or "Write it on a yellow sticky and stick it in your book so you can find it later."

Once connected through common understandings, pure theory shifts form to come into relation with the individual. Pure theory in our thinking was not permitted to derive everything from itself. It was dashed into pieces and the pieces were used to acknowledge our external conditions, our own knowledge-constitutive interests of classroom experiences, and there we found pure theory, like the Cadillac my great-grandfather treasured, to be useful.

This process of thoughtfully changing form as we are engaged in an action research methodology is sanctioned by Paille (1994). He suggests that in teacher research, an action-research methodology acknowledges the realities of daily teaching practice, the shifting and contextualized character of this practice. Action is a pivotal word. Paille believes that the addition of the word *formation* makes explicit this perception of the entwined relation of action and knowledge formation. To use the word *formation* creates an understanding of reflection that is ongoing and systematic, a reflection that we would sanction before entering into fundamental changes in our educational practices. Research and action/innovation are approved, in accord, or congruent with, and assisted by formal teaching certification, by courses, and by the work to which they are attached. The word *formation* also establishes the rhythm or the dialectic of a spiraling inquiry within a systematic, ongoing, and officially recognized pattern of questioning. Paille uses the word "*rythmées,*" which in an English translation is difficult to convey. However, the word is as critical as is his use of "formation" since both imply movement, and thus change. His is a comment on making careful, ongoing changes that are attuned to, and legitimized through, formally recognized educational practices.[2]

NO ALTAR, NO SACRIFICE

If pure theory begins to be looked upon as a treasure trove of useful parts, then it is no wonder that Leonard Cohen's question "According to whose plan?" prompts us to further questions. Questions about questions regarding pedagogical presence would have to be grounded through our lived experiences of pedagogical relations with young children. The method of questions and answers would take on the pattern of a spiral—a nonlinear and multidimensional process of shifts between phenomenological thinking, that is, the grounded lived experience of the classroom and school, the hermeneutic or interpretive resonance of experience with language, and the application or the return to the grounded experience.

Like the double helix of the DNA molecule, these aspects intertwine in a space/time relationship and connect through many planes. The three-dimensional image (four, if time is considered) is an image of depth and movement, a relation of time/space/flux. In this three-dimensional relation, knowledge shifts form. Habermas's (1971) concern about an "epistemology [that] has been flattened out to methodology" is avoided (p. 68). Thus, too, we avoid the "ontological illusion of pure theory . . . wanting to derive everything from itself" (Habermas, 1971, p. 314).

In a never-ending, ever-extending spiral we are never stilled with what Sartre (1992) calls "dead truths" or what Charles Taylor (1987) referred to as instrumental and atomistic understandings that leave us unconnected with life in a "struggle over the corpse of epistemology" (p. 485). It is not a question of choosing either one method or the other. It is not a question of eliminating methodologies, until the *right one* is found. It is, rather, essential to maintain a questioning from within, to maintain a to and fro within the body of knowledge that constitutes our epistemology. This play (to and fro) of reason sustains a pattern of movement through unknowing and knowing, re-formed through the questioning, reflective attitude that returns to the space/place of questioning. To search without this playful attitude would be to run the risk of what Rosen says is the danger of "reductiveness and schematism which picks away at narrative until we are left the bare bones . . . [and] stopping there or as Derrida puts it, 'stifling the force under the form'" (Rosen, 1986, p. 227).

The writing and the understanding that the teachers and I seek to share with you does not come from a place where the action or experience is that of the builder, creating something hoped to be permanent, built step-by-step from foundation to top, externally visible as a separate and identifiable entity. The dynamic, to-and-fro quality of our experience is not unlike what Hélène Cixous talks of when she writes of transforming experiences into words.

Being of a body with the river all the way to the rapids rather than with the boat, exposing yourself to this danger—this is a feminine pleasure. Sea you return to the sea, and rhythm to rhythm. And the builder: from dust to dust through his erected monuments. (Cixous, 1991, p. 57)

She suggests that we can be intimately connected to the rhythm of the organic. It is possible to be of one body with the river, where there is no control such as might be gained with a boat. We are of a body with the river. There is no boat that we have built. In the classrooms we are in the river. What we seek to share comes from this place, which, like the river, is dynamic and organic, full of risk and encounter, a place of to-and-fro relationships.

NOTES

1. Anna and her parents have allowed me to include this letter. In the conversation about this Anna asked that Frog be asked too. I did, and he gave his permission as well.

2. This translation is my own. The French text is presented here.

Le volet formation, enfin, peut-étre le plus novateur au sien dun tel projet, crée le lieu d'une réflexion extensive, systematique et prolongée, une reflexion sanctionée devant deboucher sur des changements durable au niveau d'un certain nombre de representations et de pratiques educatives. La recherche et l'action/innovations sont ainsi sanctionées, chapeautées, rythmées, nourries par un diplôme formel d'enseignement, par les cours composant, par les travaux qui y sont attaches. (Paille, 1994, p. 220)

4

SENSE AND PRESENCE IN CLASSROOMS

SIX SENSES

In this chapter, aspects of what it is to be pedagogically present are revealed and described as resonating, recurring, and embodied experiences of many discrete senses. To return to Cixous's metaphor of the river, these discrete aspects of presence may be likened to boulders in the riverbed. As the white water rushes over them, you know they are there. Through spumes of spray and rollers you become acutely aware of their presence. These boulders make the river what it is. Without these parts—the boulders, the ledges, the eddies, the shallows—this river would be another river, not this one. Jumping in, leaving the raft and joining the river, feet first, initially you are not quite of a body with the river, more like a log (or stick) tossed and pulled. But soon, as awareness of the rhythm, the pull, and the flow assumes form in this embodied experience, you begin to know how to move so that you can direct yourself to the riverbank. Your embodied being has *read the river*, and you have responded within the moving, shifting, and dynamic forms of river and body.

In schools, teachers watch and listen and question, a reading in a sense, of the experience of being in schools. Teachers in conversation describe the *teacher look*, the *teacher voice*. Teachers tell and retell stories, listening to our own stories and others' stories, retelling memories and re-forming ideas about how to respond today. Teachers move close to and away from the children, watch their faces, and tell the children that they need to watch our faces. Voices matter. "Oh!" a colleague cried out one day coming into the staff room. "I can't stand it! There's my teacher voice again! Yuk!" And when there is no voice, either teacher or child, that matters too. Teachers know all kinds of silences, the reading kind when the group is enthralled and the kind that parents too worry about—the "something must be going on because I don't hear anything" kind of silence.

Making sense of pedagogical presence takes form as these qualities of memory, touch, face, voice, and silence are articulated. Examples are shown here in parts. However, this is not how the teachers who told the stories experienced them. Being there was not experienced in discrete qualities, nor dare we name them themes. To name these experiences as themes would be to risk objectifying the experience, falling into the pattern of thinking that dichotomizes subject/object, even while claiming to recognize subject. To name them *themes* would remove them from the flow of life that surrounds them and would still the movement that gives them their quality of life—like the boulders in the river, once removed, they would simply be large rocks without the quality to disrupt and influence the power of the flow that surrounds them. One day when my colleague Grace and I were talking about routines and the rhythm of interactions with the children, she explained that establishing a rhythm for her meant a "putting together."

> You cannot teach without putting it all together. It's a flow, it's continuous, it's not a thematic thing, but webbing as we do themes is a way to put it altogether. I can see people interpreting rhythm as a thematic thing. I never thought of it as theme. I'd never on your life thought of it as a theme. For me it's a continuous thing.

I believe that Caputo (1987) expresses the risk of fragmentation and objectifying experience when he says, "Thematicism is a violence exerted by philosophical criticism which, for metaphysical reasons, subordinates the structure of writing and textuality to the rule of meaning. . . . The signifier is not the embodiment of meaning . . . but the power which produces meaning" (p. 150). Caputo means that any necessity to name themes makes it necessary to determine meaning. Meaning then assumes dominance. Again, as we so often do when we get a good idea, we risk cutting ourselves off from any other possibilities. It may be more helpful if we risk instead, the openness of meaning, and if we explore meaning through the power of language, rather than *capture* meaning within the bounds of language. The difference may be subtle, but I believe it is significant because language must be more than a tool. To discover meaning, to resist the desire to capture that meaning in naming, is to discover that we remain in a relationship with language that enables us to sustain the power of language to reveal, to change. This is an organic power, with the characteristics of what Grace described as a continuous flow. It is not the category or theme that establishes meaning, but the connected association and experience. Process, not product, assumes dominance. Meaning may change. To grasp, to capture, may endanger the dynamic form that characterizes what I have just come to understand. For as long as we grasp, we hold an organic quality static, and thus create a contradiction, a paradox, that puts our whole experience at risk. To grasp, to hold static, is not a quality of living with young children.

In this chapter, language retains this organic quality. It is important to know that we are exploring on the back of language, so to speak. It is as if language were a winged dragon of mythology and we are riding on its back. With access to the power of myth and mystery, we gain access to places unimagined. What follows is a description of our experience, a description that we discover is not the container of meaning, but the power through which we produce meaning.

A SENSE OF THE PAST: REMEMBERING

It was Stephanie, my principal in my third year of teaching, my first mentor, who taught me to look for meaning in remembering. Even after she retired, we would meet for lunch or coffee. One day she began to tell me a story told to her by a friend in one of her first years of teaching. During a parent-teacher interview, a mother of one of the children in the first-grade class said that her child could read, and asked how he was doing. Even though Stephanie had told me this story before, I didn't interrupt because I like the story and I like the way she tells it.

It is a good thing that I didn't stop her because in this retelling I learned something new. While I listened, I wondered why this story was so important to her that she was telling it again. She always has something she is leading me to, even though she sometimes says she hasn't thought about it until we start talking. All the way through the story I wondered. She told how her friend listened in surprise and silence to the child's mother, and then watched and talked to the child for the next few days. Then Stephanie came to the part where she always pauses and looks straight at me, with eyes widened, and she repeats her friend's words. "And all those months I didn't know that!" Each time she tells the story, her voice and face, the intensity of her gaze, all force this realization across the table, into my listening space. Each time I respond with genuine concerned and surprised attention. Each time I understand a little differently, and carry away another image of the experience of listening.

Stephanie always used to ask me the same question whenever I would ask her a question. She would respond with another question that was inevitably, "Well, what did she [or he] mean?" "Well," I ask myself now, "What does she mean?" (She and I have shared conversations about speaking two languages. She says she thinks that speaking more than one language makes a person look for meaning around the words. It is a habit she says.)

As I sat across the table and questioned, "What does she mean?" I thought about the meaning around her words. She has told me this story many times. What meaning lies in the retelling? As I waited and wondered, Stephanie asked herself aloud, "What was my friend doing?" Her voice fell and she said more quietly, "She was teaching the curriculum. She didn't even know the child could read." As I listened, it was as if she said to me, "Remember the past as I tell it to you, and remember the future as you may create it. We may or may not create opportunities for children's learning. These are the possibilities of our future."

My colleagues' stories are remembered moments that surround and intersect today's moments. We awaken in the present moment, to the now and the past. Our awakening is Proustian or embodied, entwined without beginning or end. As Marcuse (1978) points out, "There will be no end, only a remembrance of things past" (p. 48). We stand between, listening on both sides, connected with past and possibilities. We stand and talk in doorways, in hallways, at the photocopier, or the fridge, the coffeemaker, or the microwave. Where else can you capture a few moments with your colleagues? The storytelling in these spaces and places is reminiscent of the kind of action-oriented self-understanding that Habermas (1971) suggests makes it possible for us to maintain the connection between our own life stories that carry the tradition of our childhood, and the stories and traditions of many individuals, groups, and cultures.

Remembering is so much a part of the experience of living each day that it hardly seems worthwhile to consider. There is nothing unusual about remembering. It becomes unusual if we do not remember! In our classrooms, however, it is not a linear remembering that unfolds before us. A teacher's remembering folds and twists time. In seconds it is possible to experience a twist of time that presents our own childhood to us in the here and now as we see, hear, smell, or touch something that reminds us. In a minute, the time before us can contain our own childhood. This phenomenological remembering of our life experiences, then and now, sometimes helps us know what to do, what decisions to make in any of those hundreds of moments that require a decision. For example, memories of avoiding the cold at recess came up one day when two of us were on noon-hour supervision. A colleague wanted us to know about two little girls from her class who had been telling different teachers different stories each recess and noon hour when it was time to go outside. It was a cold winter day and the girls did not want to go out. The day before this story, they told the lunchroom supervisor that they could stay in, thinking she would not ask their teacher if that was so. Sherry, their teacher, saw the girls indoors and told them they must go outside. Sherry stopped Grace and me in the staff room as we were getting ready to go out on supervision. She wanted us to know about the two girls. Sherry said, "They might tell you they had permission to stay in. They *do not* have permission." She told us this with emphasis. But that was not enough for her to say. She continued with some anecdotes about the girls' classroom behaviors, and how she responded to those. They would "get up to mischief while seeming at first glance to have no responsibility for initiating anything out of line." Sherry knew that if she told Grace this, it would help Grace to ensure that her responses would be consistent with Sherry's past responses. Yet even this was not enough for Sherry to be confident that Grace really understood what Sherry did about the girls.

She continued, "At first glance they look innocent, but if you watch more closely you can see them looking sideways at those who are acting out of line. I know this look! I used to do this as child! My main purpose in school was to get others into trouble." Grace now knew that "these girls couldn't be *that* bad" if Sherry could talk about their behaviors with laughter and reminders that she too had been much like these children.

Sherry laughed and added, "And Grace, of course, probably didn't get into *any* mischief!" Sherry and Grace have taught together long enough to have shared many stories of their own childhood experiences. Sherry knows from these stories how hard Grace struggled as child in a private girls' school to find ways to get into mischief.

All Sherry's information was conveyed in about four minutes. For such a seemingly simple matter as noon-hour supervision, we quickly fold past, present, and future into our storytelling. We do this because we can, and because we have an interest in the girls' behavior and responses to us. We choose to use our time in this way. We claim some fragment of time because "this vast dimension which I had not known myself to possess" (Proust, 1981, p. 106) is useful in our planning and discipline strategies. Time is thick and malleable, enabling the folding of moment over moment, so that one brief glance of the present may touch another, older glance, at the same moment as we reach out to touch the possible future. We bring with us to our noon-hour supervision "the *remembered* child . . . [a structure of time] which Merleau-Ponty called 'transitional synthesis,' the binding of past and future in the presence field of present" (Lippitz, 1986, p. 56).

Our sense of time is embodied, elusively possessed, and articulated through the ways of our being in schools. For example, on the work-table, in someone's bin of "stuff to do before class" is a book that catches my eye. Perhaps it is the illustration on the front that catches my eye—a smiling but rather droopy-looking older woman grips the arms of a wicker chair while a young boy skateboards out from behind the chair. This scene looks familiar. Here is a part of my personal experience—I remember my youngest son on inline skates in the dining room, just like the illustration on the cover. And I felt the same as the old woman in the rocking chair looks! The title offers no inspirational clue—*Wilfred Gordon McDonald Partridge*. My curiosity is noticed (not hard to do since I am already reaching for the book) and the book's owner becomes effusively excited. "You have to have it! It's about memories! This old woman has lost her memory and the boy helps her find it. Read it, you'll see. You can borrow it when I'm finished." What is this sense of remembering that so excited my colleague? In the story, Wilfred Gordon hears his parents saying that his favorite person in the old people's home next door to him was a "poor old thing because she's lost her memory" (Fox, 1984, unpaginated).

> "What's a memory?" asked Wilfred Gordon.
> "It is something you remember," said his father. But the boy wanted to know more, so he called on Mrs [sic] Jordan who played the organ.
> "What's a memory?" he asked.
> "Something warm, my child, something warm." (Fox, 1984)

The sense of time that held meaning for Wilfred Gordon was an embodied, possessed-in-the-hands meaning. He searched for something warm, and "took a fresh, warm egg from under a hen." Asking and listening, Wilfred Gordon heard that memories were "something from a long time ago, me lad," "something that makes you cry," "something that makes you laugh," and "something as precious as gold." His desire to offer a lost memory to Miss Nancy led him in search of a shoebox of shells, the medals his grandfather had given him, a puppet on a string, his precious football. He gave these to Miss Nancy.

> Miss Nancy reached out to touch the egg and told Wilfred Gordon about the tiny speckled blue eggs she had once found in a bird's nest in her aunt's garden.
> She put a shell to her ear and remembered going to the beach by tram long ago and how hot she had felt in her button-up boots. . . . And the two of them smiled and smiled. (Fox, 1984)

This is the sense of time teachers claim and share. We share through stories, our own and others'. Time is a sense of being, of desire, of reaching to touch, of seeing and hearing. Unless entwined through then and now, into the future of desire, memory is a lost thing, and we are poorer for it.

There are many opportunities to know what remembering sounds and looks like in schools and classrooms. Again, in a school workroom, when asked one day what I was doing and how things were going, I responded with my usual few comments about still wondering how to put *pedagogical presence* into words. My colleague had no such apparent hesitation. He started right in and said, "For me, presence is having to awaken." Standing by the worktable, he went on to tell me about how he remembers what he called his "first awakening." Teaching in an "inner-city school—not, you know the kind of inner-city school where the children of immigrants go, the other kind," he "had a Grade 1/2 combined class of 37 children. Fifty-two kids went through that class that year." Story followed story. His gaze was intense as he told me about a seven-year-old child's drawings of parking meters beside beds. He said, "The child, a seven-year-old child, said to me 'My mother's a whore.'" "Awakening," he said, "happens over and over again. It's not just something that you can think about and know." He shrugged his shoulders, his hands facing palm upward. What can he say, and how can he say it? There is no end to knowing, and to forms of knowing. Years later, after his first awakening, here he is, as he says, "awakening, over and over."

Here, in the workrooms of our schools, we awaken and reawaken to memories that we carry here with us. Memories can be carried, as Wilfred Gordon carried the shoebox to Miss Nancy, and as my colleague did through the embodied shrug of the shoulder, palms up. Memories can be expansively extended through the time and space between us, through a voice, and with a shared visual image. Our sense of time is thus not a plane of discrete linear sequences, but is an organic perception in which is enfolded the past, the present, and the hopes of the future.

Memories and time are not discrete, even though the words themselves are separate and have a discrete meaning. It is through a poet's language that we see and hear the shifting shape of the discrete and separated word. In *For the Sake of a Single Poem*, Rilke (1989) shows us the illusion and the paradox of our reason. It is Rilke (1989) who invokes an image of the body/mind to re-mind us that we are embodied thought and language, and it is this embodied quality that makes meaning.

> For the sake of a single poem one must see many cities, many people and Things. . . . And it is not yet enough to have memories. You must be able

to forget them when they are many, and you must have the immense patience to wait until they return. For the memories themselves are not important. Only when they have changed into our very blood, into glance and gesture, and are nameless, no longer to be distinguished from ourselves—only then can it happen that in some very rare hour the first word of a poem arises in their midst and goes forth from them. (p. 91)

It is not enough for us to have memories. It is not the memories themselves that are important. In schools, memory is that which is both remembered and forgotten, there, but not seen, turned to blood under our skin. It is glance and gesture, face and hands, heart, gut, and blood. Rilke's image of embodied knowing, integrated into our being, sometimes unacknowledged, forgotten for a while, is described by Palmer (1998) as "a mystic's map of wholeness, where inner and outer reality flow seamlessly into each other, like the ever-merging surfaces of a Mobius strip, endlessly co-creating us and the world we inhabit" (p. 5).

Often we do not know how to say what we cannot even remember to say; and it is not always because we are suffering from what my sons call early Alzheimer's when they want to tease me! No, it is that we often find it difficult to distinguish thought from self. We simply know, we just cannot say. Our words, our thoughts, our memories, as Polanyi (1958) suggests, disappear like sugar dissolved in the tea. Perhaps this is what characterizes wisdom, when experience and knowing become one— embodied within a multitude of moments, each of those embodied within another, until, like the Russian doll, we see the knowing and do not see the smaller experiences nested within. Perhaps it is this that often frustrates both student teacher and teacher as they struggle to work together. The teacher no longer can identify and articulate what she (or he) knows, any more than she can articulate how she moves her body in order to stand up.

HOPING AND EXPECTING

A chance meeting with a teacher at a social gathering led me to think that hope and expectation as an aspect of our remembering should be included in our understanding of pedagogical presence. The teacher at the gathering expressed her unwillingness to teach at a school where the students were of another cultural background, where there was "no appreciation for someone who was interested in working at a school level in an area of specialty." The teacher said she was at her current school only because nothing better was available. I listened, saying little. The teacher and parent in me listened. My youngest son is a child of what this teacher describes as "another cultural background." In me, images of past and present enfolded around a vision of my son's future, my hopes and desires for him. I felt fear and apprehension, and anger that he might be excluded from a teacher's willingness to teach him.

As frustrating as the conversation was to me personally, however, I began to understand in real terms that the selection of people with whom I was working to develop an understanding of pedagogical presence (those to whom I spoke in beginning conversations, those old friends I met in parking lots and at trade shows at conventions) was indeed a selection. Just as I have had the opportunity throughout most of my career to make reasonable choices regarding those colleagues with whom I would like to work, I have made choices regarding those involved in this questioning process. Certainly many of my first conversations were not with people I sought out and arranged to talk with. They were with colleagues I just happened to see. When I see an old friend on the street, I call out hello, or they do, and thus begins our conversation. If we were not friends, we would not have called out to each other. We joke about the possibilities of chance meetings and mutual friends and longevity in what we call *the system*, and this too becomes part of the conversation.

Helen, another of my colleagues, points out that both of us have chosen not to associate with colleagues who express views such as those described above. "What does she expect? Only to work at schools where there are no kids like *that*?" Helen snuffs. "Humph! I don't even like to stay in the staff room when conversations get like that." This is not to say that Helen avoids confronting issues, but she uses her professional judgment when choosing appropriate situations for challenge, just as we do with children.

We hope and we expect that we will find ways to teach all children, just as, if we are parents, we hope that our children will have teachers who will help them to learn. Confronted with the reality of these hopes and expectations, an administrator with whom I worked once said "If they're conscious, they can be here!" Years later, this man was honored by hundreds of parents, children, and former staff with a candlelight vigil outside his hospital window a few weeks before his death. There was a need to honor him, to acknowledge that his presence was significant and would be missed. The lights of the candles were intended to share the quality of acute and sensitive awareness, as he had with us, an awareness of the significance of being present with each other.

We expect there will be difficulties and fears. Past experience cautions us that there probably will not be enough funding required to cover the school costs of the children who are designated as having special needs. However, in spite of inadequate funding and large classes, my colleague at the photocopier keeps coming back, year after year, still awakening. And me? I put the poster of Lucy up again, the one drawn by Schultz, with Lucy sitting in her school desk, the caption saying "Here I am again, looking for the answers."

We find some answers in the moments taken to talk with each other, as we did at noon hour that day that Sherry was concerned about the two little girls who were trying to stay in out of the cold at noon. Our conversations touch a deep and distant mischief in our remembering, and we expect we may see the same in these little girls as we saw in ourselves long ago. But will there also be a remembrance forward? Or is this what we might call thinking about the future, a hoping for the future—our desire? Perhaps the words of Ricoeur (1991) clarify the meaning. In his book *From Text to Action*, he writes about the *"horizon of expectation,"* which is

> Broad enough to include hope and fear, wishing and willing, care, rational calculation, curiosity—in short, all manifestation, whether private or communal, relating to the future. Like experience, the expectation of the future is inscribed in the present; it is *future-become-present*, turned toward the not-yet. (p. 218)

The horizon of expectation opens out, encompassing the past experience and the future in a to-and-fro play, within this moment, this place, this relation—present and here, yet immanent.

We reach the depth of the past from the stance of the now, and know that our personal knowledge of teaching is not unidimensional or flat. Our expectations and hopes are the future, touching past and now. It is difficult to separate the many dimensions. For example, my colleague who says that she will "keep hoping, although I should know better" that one day she will not have so much work to do and that she will have no children with challenging behaviors in her class. Her present is the paradoxical experience of hope re-creating possibility for hope.

Sometimes, when we cannot do this for ourselves, we need the opportunity for conversation with colleagues who share the paradoxical experience of hope re-creating hope. Helen provided that opportunity for me one day. She interrupted my expressions of dismay over my inability to understand what a child was telling me through his actions. I could not understand this child's behavior! I was forgetting to remember, and thus could not re-create hope. But Helen reminded me. As we talked, she reminded me that we have both had to learn about children's learning in situations where language was not a possibility, and that we had been able to do it. She reminded me that we had to rely on whatever we could to discover meaning when we were working with severely disabled and autistic children. She reminded me that these children unknowingly taught us how to watch for the language of the body, of the face, the eyes, and the touch. I understood then that I had to stop being frustrated because words were not there; the child was not going to tell me. I would not have the words I was searching for, so I had to quit looking for what could not be replayed in time! Helen was helping me to look again for what was there, and to try again to *see* what the child was doing. She asked me, "How was he moving, where? What about his hands, feet, face, eyes?" Through her questions she was showing me that there was hope. I would be able to figure it out if I just kept thinking and remembering and talking with my colleagues.

There are moments and days when it is tempting to avoid these dilemmas, not simply to call in sick, but to speak with anger and resentment, as one of my colleagues did one day close to spring break, exclaiming, "What more do they want of us! The parents are just not realizing we need to have a life!" Another colleague says she sometimes comes close to becoming unhinged. We have spent entire lunch breaks howling with laughter at the moments when we thought our teaching practice, our very selves, were becoming unhinged. Laughter is easy when the moment of not knowing whether or not we would be able to cope has passed. I can laugh now about how I had to take two gulps of antacid each morning before leaving for work. That was before I had a classroom aide for the child with a severe behavioral disorder. My colleague can laugh now when she tells about being eight months pregnant, the sole adult responsible on a field trip with a group of students with special needs in the days before we took cell phones with us on field trips. One of the children became aggressive and she had to restrain him and at the same time call the school for help from a pay phone. (She sat on him!) My colleague laughs so hard the tears form in her eyes, saying it must have been a pretty funny sight to see this very pregnant woman struggling with a child at least as big as she was. She expresses no expectation that someone should have helped her, or resentment that she was expected to be able to cope on her own with the children. We just "keep hoping," knowing "it's never easy." We make a choice to be present, learning from those situations that are difficult and sharing our learning with our colleagues. Stephanie says,

> You have a choice. You want to or you don't. It depends on how deeply inquisitive you are, if you are curious to see. Some people have the expectation of children to be so adult-like. When they behave so child-like, not like small adults, people don't want to see them. [She laughed.] It's not always so good to be an adult!

We have chosen to be with children in a relationship that is also part of our childhood experience, a part of the past. "'Presence,' of course, is not only an experience of our spatiality; it is also an experience that is deeply rooted in the temporality of our vision" (Levin, 1988, p. 456). Presence is paradoxically located in the past as well as in the present. Can we remember what it was to be a child? We are here in the now, but time has traveled here with us.

Levin's comment affirms what my colleagues are suggesting as we attempt to understand what *pedagogical presence* means. The sense of time that constitutes one aspect of pedagogical presence is constituted through our experiences of self, other, an awareness of time (then now and-what-next), pictorial images of children's literature, colleagues' gestures, photocopy machine hum, and of words said and meanings unsaid.

What we have known, what we hope, and what we expect, all help us to create and re-create (sometimes with humor) what we have known, in an impossibly entwined and seemingly never-ending sequence. Enough becomes enough over and over. (Until sometimes some of my colleagues "go half time just to survive," or take long-term stress leave.)

REACHING AND TOUCHING

Sitting at a staff meeting of a combined elementary-junior high school, listening to a discussion of the possible implications of a female junior high student's accusations regarding inappropriate touching, led me to realize what I had taken for granted in relations with younger children. When I stopped to think about what my practice would be like if I were not able to touch a child, I could not imagine what my day would look like.

This is a dilemma I had briefly discussed with colleagues in larger gatherings, at professional association meetings, conventions, or seminars. Generally the topic arose only if a situation had been in the media. The teachers with whom I worked in primary classrooms seldom gave thought to the concept of touching or not touching. It was another of the things they just do. As one said, "I couldn't teach without touching. Maybe high school teachers have to worry about that, I can certainly see that, but us?"

Touching Gopher Holes

Touching was part of our hands-on learning. In our classrooms, touching was something that happened as part of the entire teaching-learning process. For example, Helen told me of her experience on a field trip to a nature center. She and a child's parent stood by the grass watching the child kneeling down to poke his head into a gopher hole. The rest of the group went on with the tour guide. The parent expressed concern that the child was "always like this, poking his head into things and not going with the group." However, the parent did not want to discourage the child's intimate investigation of the world. Parent and teacher were aware of the relationship between the child's kneeling at the entrance to the gopher hole and the child's knowing. They watched as language and knowing touched each other in the space surrounding the gopher hole.

The Pumpkin Story

Similar experiences occur in the classroom. For example, one day Helen put several pumpkins on a table at the science center. I watched and listened and questioned.

The pumpkin sits on the table, its top removed, revealing the unknown, inviting exploration. The children respond. Some children spread themselves across the table as they stretch their necks like turtles to reach inside the pumpkin. How essential is it for that child to get so close to the inside of a pumpkin that his face is almost inside it? Couldn't he wait until I passed it closer to him? Is this how he learns? How necessary is it for him to have this immediate, intimate experience of smell, and touch, and sight? It is really frustrating not knowing what to do right now. The table is pretty stable. I don't think he'll fall off or tip it over. I stand watching for a few seconds, then I pull both child and pumpkin to the edge of the table, so that his feet slide onto the floor. I don't think he even notices me moving him!

Reading *Charlotte's Web*

I watched and listened again as Helen read *Charlotte's Web* to the class of five- and six-year-olds. Two children wriggle up each side of the chair, hands winding snakelike up the rounded steel sides. The teacher reaches out with one hand to help the child climb into her lap, supporting another child's arm with her back. Wrapped around with arms and book, the child smiles from this encircled space, looking out at the other children. She says, "You turn the page, I'll tell you when." The child leans into her. I see a child's head alternately nestled in the space between the teacher's head and shoulder, then lift intently toward the page. Sometimes the teacher's view of the words is blocked, but the child is intense with concentration, a face glowing with pleasure. Hovering over the teacher's shoulder, breathing in her space, leaning on the back of the chair, arm supported against his teacher's back, another child looks out over the group. If eyes can smile, this child's eyes are smiling—focused on nothing that I can identify, the child seems to gaze serenely to nowhere in particular, then laughs when Wilbur's trough is knocked over, and laughs again when the animals are offended by the odor of Templeton's egg as it wafts across the barnyard.

Children touch and are touched. They reach out to touch their world, and when their world responds to assist this reaching, they reach out further. There are approximately 85 uses of the word *touch* in the Oxford Dictionary. Definitions and descriptions take up almost two columns. Obviously this is a word that conjures up a multitude of meanings. In this book, we understand touch to mean something closer to Carse's description. Touch, says Carse (1986), is "reciprocal" (p. 75).

> Touch is more than proximity, touch is responsive and reciprocal.
>   Touch is a characteristically paradoxical phenomenon of infinite play. . . . Touching is always reciprocal. You cannot touch me unless I touch you in response . . . whoever touches me is touched as well. . . . We are touched through our veils. (Carse, 1986, p. 75)

Touch is a to-and-fro play with infinite possibilities—an infinite game. To touch is not the same as to move. To move requires force applied toward another, and that would not be a reciprocal act. The children reach out to touch the pumpkin. You could say that the pumpkin responds, yielding its cool, smooth texture and the scent of Halloweens to come. Children reach out to touch the teacher who reads the story, and they are touched in a response that reaches into the child's knowledge of what it is to share the intimacy of storytelling with a parent.

Carse's veil is a permeable membrane delineating an elusive boundary between self and other. Through such boundaries we reach out to touch and are touched. Helen's shoulder touches the child and the child's head touches her. Space *for* each is made *from* each. Without the reciprocal act of touch, we would cease to reach out into the world beyond ourselves. The kind of touching that the junior high school teachers were concerned about in the staff meeting was not the kind of touch that we think of when reading to young children, or rescuing them from the possibility of landing on the floor, squashed under a pumpkin that has fallen on top of them.

Even voice can touch through that elusive boundary between self and other. Adele Wiseman (1956) in *The Sacrifice* masks the wisdom of this consciousness with the madness of Abraham. Abraham tells his grand-son who visits him for the first time in the institution for the mentally ill: "In her voice were the voices of the children. Do not harm her, lest you hear them weeping" (p. 344). It seems to his family that Abraham has gone mad. He has been touched by an awareness that he cannot bear. His being resonates with the knowing of those who have suffered more than he is able to know.

Wiseman suggests that only through madness can we endure the knowledge that we are the voice of the one in the other. She is suggest-ing that through voice we touch. (It used to be said that the mad were *touched*.) Be careful, Wiseman hints, because your voice will touch what you cannot see, and you may be touched by what you cannot see. In classrooms our boundaries are chosen and not chosen, visible and invisi-ble. Children and teacher, through voice, eyes, and gesture, reach to touch, desiring to know.

VOICE: SNOW PILES AND STAFF ROOMS

What is "voice" in the classroom? What is the relationship between voice and pedagogical presence?

A male voice booms across the playground, "No!" The sound carries across wet snow piles, and those children at the base of a snow pile, where the iced puddle meets the snow pile, stop. The teacher and I who have come out to join our colleague on supervision look at each other as we watch the children respond to the booming "No!" We smile be-cause we do not have to walk across the playground to that iced puddle. Our female voices would not have carried as far as our colleague's deep male voice. There will be no more small feet creaking across the ice to set the water free, and no more teary, soaked, and frozen children to care for. And we will not have to try to be in two places at once to keep the children off the ice, while watching all the others.

This event prompts us to talk about how we hear ourselves. Helen laughs and says she sometimes sounds silly. I remind her of what I heard from the children today when we gathered on the carpet.

Teacher: "You can't giggle today! Only on Friday!"
Children: (giggling)
Child: "Mrs. Paul's giggling—it's only Wednesday!"

Sometimes our voices boom across the playground, and sometimes they join the children in a playful exchange. A story like this can also be told in a language that is seldom heard in classrooms, but that means much the same.

> Life in the classroom is not so much *in* the child, *in* the teacher, *in* the subject; life is lived in the spaces between and among . . . in the intertextual spaces of inter-faces, the places where "betweens" and "and's" [*sic*] reside, the spaces where "and" is no mere conjoining word but more so a place of difference, where something different can happen or be created' [*sic*] where whatever is created comes through as a voice that grows in the middle. This voice is the sound of the "interlude" (inter/ludus—to play), the voice of play in the midst of things—a playful singing in the midst of life. (Aoki, 1993, p. 69)

Some teachers may believe that Ted Aoki is being a little idealistic when he writes this way. Teachers do not always feel as if their voices are "a playful singing." In the classroom, says Grace, "sometimes that's my teacher voice. Yuk." Sometimes we do not like the sound of ourselves. Sometimes our voice is a sigh of exhaustion and dismay. A teacher angrily said in the staff room one day,

> How can we take them there? We can't ask the parents for more money than it costs to go on one field trip! You know, I have four kids coughing in my class this morning and one with her head on her desk and one with a note to take on the field trip so Grandma can come—and that's halfway across the city—to pick up Sam if he gets too sick! It's not even glorified babysitting any more, there's no glory in it!

We alternate between the differences of self and other, between the playful giggling of negotiating a shared space/time for child and teacher voice, and the grim voice of exhaustion. Our intention is to create the voice that grows in the middle. For this, I listen to Helen. I watch her with the children. She says she would like to create a space for the children's voices.

One of the things I'd like to create is the opportunity for them [the children] just to talk. I don't even know what it would look like. We'd come together and talk, but I'm worried that would be contrived, because what they need is to speak, to be up and in control of the dialogue. And the two groups have a different feel to them. In the afternoon, with the kindergarten children there, the group has different characteristics.

You have to play with it. I also don't know if I have the energy, so I'm playing with it and I've got to find other ways to teach this, and I've got to play and work with other things too.

I listened to Helen say this again and again on an audiotape I had made of our conversation. Listening, I could see her in my mind's eye, in the middle of a group of children. On tape I hear her saying she wants to create an opportunity for the children to talk. Through notes and in my memory I see her again, sitting at a small table with only four children, leaning forward, so close to the children that if she moved her head suddenly, she and a child might collide. The tone I hear through the tape echoes over the scene in my mind's eye. Other voices mingle, louder, softer, some I am unable to recall. Sounds echo, replaying the past in the present, layers of time and sound. Just as I experienced when I sat with Anna, as she invited Frog to come to her world, again I experience the creation of sound-sense. Slowly meaning becomes visible through text and sound and rememberings of the moves and language of the teacher and the children.

Is Helen not already creating an opportunity for the children to talk through her listening presence? In staff-room conversations she tells me it is important for her to make time to be with a small group of children. In the classroom I watch as she moves to create environments and opportunities for small groups to be together, and as she moves to sit with them. This looks to me as if she has created an opportunity for the children just to talk, and I wonder—does she see the same thing now that we begin to talk and reflect? Being the "writer/researcher," I have time to listen to what has already been said, to reread the scribbled notes. This form of questioning/recollection has again those familiar qualities of picking up in the classroom at the end of the day as I re collect those fragments of conversation and children's work that we have been reluctant to discard. Laughing to myself, I make the analogy of portfolio assessment to the methodology of our questioning process. I see that we cannot stop acting like teachers because, just as I stuff impromptu and informal fragments of children's daily activities, as well as accomplished, polished bits, into the children's folders, so I have stuffed the polished, taped conversations and scribbled notes into the matter comprising this questioning process.

Later we talked about the structuring of opportunities for children to express themselves. For example, Helen believed that the criteria for testing and grading achievement of children's writing restricted possibilities for the children to learn to express themselves. Our question about voice in the classroom led us from the intimacy of playful humor, and the perplexity of developing the children's expressive dialogue skills, to a defense of these voices. Helen believed we need to create opportunities for children to experience a valuing of their expressive abilities without the excessive restraints that some evaluative processes impose.

I believe that Helen's criticism of some mandated evaluative procedures was a defense of the "play of reason against the principle of reason ... [because] to take the play out of reason would reduce reason to dead seriousness" (Caputo, 1987, p. 227). She was prepared to create a space and time for the children to develop their conversational abilities. She was prepared to play with strategies to enable this in the classroom. We talked about some of the current assessment tools we were required by school board and provincial policies to use, and we talked about some of the reading I had been doing. I read to Helen the following note I had written in my journal.

> Are we taking what Caputo called the risks of "non-institutionalised reason" (Caputo, 1987) the kind of reason that gets mucked about by the hands-on approach of young children who stick their heads into pumpkins and gopher holes—or do we leave the children with those who deal in Sartre's (1992) dead truths and teach curriculum, not children?

Helen responded that she thought dead truths were what the exercise felt like. "Where will this child's writing find someone who will value it if we have to use these criteria?" she asked as she read to me a piece of writing in which a child used imagery to convey a memory of a day at the beach. It did not include a descriptive sentence, and so it did not meet the standard, and thus became rated as *adequate*. Helen could find no space for the child's voice in this assessment of skills. The assessment tool that we were required to use was designed to assess particular skills. Those skills did not include aspects of young children's expressive voices that Helen valued, such as the ability to create imagery through a linguistic structure that resembled free verse.

Helen's argument to support the creation of space and time to enable children to develop their voices is similar to what Aoki says about voice. As he suggested, voice is not *in*, voice is situated where there is a space of interlude, where possibilities can be created for to-and-fro relations between and among children, teacher, and curriculum.

As I attempt to understand the relationship between voice and pedagogical presence, and as I listen to Helen continue to return to the child's voice, and her role in encouraging that voice, I keep hearing about a person, that is, the child or the teacher. I recall Anna again, and the sound, singing, sense-making of her letter writing to Frog. Persons and sound resonate, making per-son-a, us, our presence is embodied.

It is interesting to read that the word *person* in the *Oxford English Dictionary* (1933) comes from a word that has two parts, per-sona, and per-sonare. In this word we see, though do not hear, a difference between our understandings of the word *person* as we now use it, and the way it may have been understood. "Sona, sonare" and the French "sonner" (to ring) ring in my ear as I look at the words. Caputo (1987) describes this meaning as

> the person sounding through, resonating. This pre-Cartesian word does not name a seat of self identity. . . . On the contrary, it means to name a difference, to pick up the interplay between mask and voice, face and speech, look and language, *eidos* and *logos* (p. 289).

"Embedded in the metaphorics of the flux . . . *per-sona* [is] the opening through which the flux resonates" (Caputo, 1987, p. 290). In this statement, we hear again Aoki's understanding of voice as sound in the interlude, sound resonating, an interplay of persons through the flux.

Person, in this sense, now reminds us of the embodied sense of our person/being. We are present, and we feel that which we hear. Voice resonates through the boundaries of skin and language (sound), touch-

ing and being touched. Child or teacher, our voices are embodied, resonating through the space between, a shifting presence of self and other,
teacher, child(ren), and curriculum.

SILENCE

I appreciate the way that Adrienne Rich (1978) describes silence. It is,
she says, "a presence" with a history and a form. We are not to "confuse
it with any kind of absence" (p. 17). She cautions us to be careful. Do
not think that silence means no voice. I learned this from a friend, an
experienced teacher who helped me during my first year of teaching.
One day she told me about a visit to a friend she hadn't seen for a long
time. "We just sat there on the steps at the front door. He didn't say
much. But I knew what he meant outside the words." My friend's first
language is Cree, and the friend she was visiting also spoke Cree as his
first language. They understood that silence is not an absence. Silence
requires thought. Silence offers possibility for thought. The whole of
understanding requires silence. Through silence he spoke to her, and
she understood, like Barthes (1985) who said, "My reading remains sus-
pended between the image and its description, between definition and
approximation. . . . The obtuse meaning is *outside* [italics added] (articulated) language, but still within interlocution. . . . We do without speech
yet continue to understand each other" (p. 55). Outside the words, my
friend knew that silence is not absence of voice. Perhaps it is only our
Western ways that make it necessary to talk about silence.

Caputo (1987) also cautions us to be aware of the relationship between silence and meaning. "The one thing necessary is that this dialogue issue from originary saying itself and that it remain suitable
reticent, free of chatter, silent even about silence" (p. 107). I know that
I can natter on at school with the children, and my words are simply
there to fill a silence. It is the silence that is sometimes full of meaning,
more than the "nattering." In schools we are generally silent about our
own silence. We seldom have to think about how to make it intelligible
to each other. We are like parents who share a meaningful gaze when
suddenly there is no noise. We say to ourselves, "Something must be
going on because I don't hear anything!" No words are necessary—only

action. We expect that colleagues who work with young children will understand the character of silence in our classrooms, that it is we who are silent more than the children. It is we who try to remain free of chatter so that we are able to better understand what the children mean *outside* their words.

One day Helen was very angry with a consultant who came to assess and work with Angela, a child in her class. After Helen told me how frustrated she was, she said, "Next time I'm going to tell her to sit there and not say a word, not a word, just watch!" And she did. The next time the consultant sat and did not say a word. Later she exclaimed to Helen that she hadn't known Angela could do what she had seen and heard. She was really "surprised and glad" that she had just watched and listened. Helen said, "Of course Angela could do those things! I'd told her, but some people just can't see! They just go on thinking or doing their own thing!" In this case, the teacher's silence was essential. The teacher's silence, her quiet observation and listening, enabled possibilities for her to know more about the child.

Our own silence is only one aspect of silence in the classroom. We know of the possibilities for another aspect of silence when we read to children. For example, one morning in the kindergarten classroom I sat on a small chair, with 25 children gathered in front of me. Two at the edge of the group were looking at a book they had taken from a basket I had placed at the edge of the rug to entice them closer to the experience of listening in a group to a story. They were still engrossed when the others were ready for me to begin. I was pleased to see the two children so fascinated with these books and I did not interrupt them. It was a relief to see one of those two children coming to books now without my insistence, and to see that he was choosing books with obvious enthusiasm. He did not seem to notice what was going on around him, and I thought; "Now maybe he'll be OK with books." Three days ago, before a long weekend, I had begun to read a North Atlantic folk tale, *The Seal Mother* (Gerstein, 1986). The story is about a man out fishing in his small boat who discovered a group of seals on a rock in the early evening. The seals shed their skins and are transformed into lovely women who dance on the rock. The man stole a skin and then refused to return it to the Seal Woman to whom it belonged unless she agreed to marry him. She agreed and eventually they had a son, named Andrew. As he grew up, Andrew's mother told him stories about the ocean and animals that live in the ocean.

Before I began the remainder of the story, I looked around and I wondered if the children still wanted to finish this story. I wondered if they might have lost interest after the long weekend. Is this an important story to them? Oh well. I took a breath, scanned the group again and began. The story continued, telling how one night Andrew heard his parents arguing about the ocean and seals. Later, his mother fell asleep with her head on the table, and Andrew heard a voice from the sea, calling his name. He sneaked out past his mother and came to the edge of a cliff, from where he heard his name called. In his attempt to find a way to the bottom of the cliff, he reached inside a small hole, where he found a wrapped sealskin. He decided this must be the sealskin he has heard his parents arguing about and he returned home to his mother with the skin. He and his mother returned to the cliff.

At this moment in the story, Andrew's mother put on the sealskin and was transformed into a seal. She embraced Andrew, breathed into his lungs and together they dove off the cliff into the sea.

At this part of the story, I began to see puzzled expressions on the children's faces. I wondered if the word *embrace* was unfamiliar. Not wanting to disturb the fascination I saw, I slowed down and added another sentence to the story, saying that Andrew and his mother hug each other. Still, the children's puzzled faces looked up at me as one face. "This is unexpected, I thought." I searched for a split second for an answer, and then, unwilling to enter the children's concentration, as if talking to myself, I wondered aloud if "Perhaps all this had something to do with magic. Or with, well, what?" and my voice trailed off as I realized I didn't have a thought about "or with what." As my voice trailed off, I became aware of the silence created in the wake of my own trailing. Even the children's eyes were silent, just looking, not moving. This was a still silence that, in a kindergarten classroom, has a presence like no other; although other age groups also have their own silences, the character is not the same. From out of the still silence, Jen said, "Maybe it has something to do with love."

Silence—frozen, no breath, a breathless silence. As one we turned to Jen. I leaned forward; so close I could touch her. I spoke very quietly so as not to disturb the silence, and said very slowly, with great care, "Maybe it has something to do with love. Yes."

When I unwrapped myself from the silence and the space of the children's gaze around Jen, and moved back in the chair, I could see the other children again. We were all still and quiet. I watched the children move out of the stillness and I thought how glad I was that I had decided to continue with the story after the three days away from it. I was happy that I had found the story, and chosen to read it. As I watched a little boy who had been sitting at my feet, I realized that he had almost crawled into my lap, and I thought to myself, "Just look at him! He wants to walk right onto the pages of this book and if he doesn't move back he'll be folded right into it when I close it!"

Reluctantly, I let go of the moment and continued. I made it easier to let go by promising myself that this could happen again if I remembered to read carefully to the children, and if I tried to find stories in which the children could find this sort of respectful enchantment. "Respect?" I wondered what I meant with that thought. "Oh well, that's what it feels like, so never mind, on with it. The children are ready to go on with something more now."

Later on I was able to think about what had happened. I have always been fascinated with fairy tales. As soon as I learned to read, my father gave me two volumes of fairy tales that I read under my covers with a flashlight after I was supposed to be asleep. A friend who knows how much I enjoyed these tales, gave me a copy of *Women Who Run with the Wolves*. The author, Estés, said, "The child lives what the seal woman has breathed into him" (1992, p. 292). In a reversal of roles, Jen has breathed into me what she has lived, and thus we are able to share an understanding of the story, and of the reading, listening, storytelling experience. When a child speaks into the silence of my unknowing, the child returns to me the skin that I shed in my role of speaker and doer, returns me to my ontological being. The transformation thus opens onto connections for further knowing. Estés (1992) describes *The Seal Mother* as a

> tale told across the world, for it is an archetype, a universal knowing about an issue of soul. . . . The story tells us about where we truly come from, what we are made of, and how we must all, on a regular basis, use our instincts and find our way back home. (p. 257)

The experience of reading to the children has drawn me beyond my personal knowing, beyond the explicit knowing expressed through the formalism of the genre of folk tales, toward something real. Jen drew me to a reality that I recognized, to a reality I had once known and had forgotten. Transformation does have something to do with love. There is no magic about it. Reading to the children was an act that enabled me to understand what I did not know I knew, and this knowing came to be in the time/space of silence.

Like the stillness of Eliot's Chinese jar, moving perpetually in its stillness, silence is a space, an interval that opens onto possibilities for understanding, drawing us through the boundaries that distinguish self and other. We could not have voice without this interval of silence.

FACE TO FACE

Caputo (1987) says that the face is "the most conspicuous point of access, the outermost surface of our body, which opens the way to the recess, the 'ground' of the soul, its most hidden chambers" (p. 272). Teachers like to see children's faces—for many reasons.

I watched a child who came to his teacher and told her he had finished doing his one thing at the computer, so now wanted some free time. His eyes were twinkling and his mouth smiling. His teacher knew that the one thing he did at the computer center was to turn the computer on and off. She looked at him and smiled, her eyes matching the twinkle in his. I felt as if I were watching a conspiracy. With a conspiratorial twinkle in two pairs of eyes, what could have become a relation of energy directed toward dominance became a relation of play with unspoken language.

The teacher chose not to set up what some would call behavioral objectives for the child. Instead she saw opportunities for being with the child in the present, to share in his celebration of knowing. Weeks later, this child could be seen arguing with another, claiming more time at the computer.

On a visit to Grace's class one day, I sat at a little table as the children returned to their classroom from the art room. One of the children came straight toward me and, putting his elbows on the table, made a cradle with his hands from which his face beamed. Leaning across the table, bringing his face to mine, still beaming, eyes sparkling, he said to me, "You know, when I was painting today my teacher said it showed action," and he continued to beam from his cradled face.

It was just a little thing one teacher said as she passed his place at the table. For the other teacher too, to see the child's face, to look into his eyes and hear his voice, was just a moment, just a little thing. When I told the teachers about this event, they smiled and laughed. They said they would do this again. The child knows he has been seen. The experience for the child means,

> being confirmed as existing, as being a person and a learner. . . . A real teacher *knows* how to see children—notices a shyness, a certain mood, a feeling of expectation. Real seeing in this sense uses more than eyes. When I see a child for whom I have responsibility, I see the child with my body. In the sensory quality of my gesture, the tilt of my head, a certain bounce in my feet, my body *sees* the child's manner of starting this day, and the child experiences being seen. (van Manen, 1986, p. 21)

To be face to face helps us to see opportunities and possibilities, and to hope. It enables us to live in pedagogic relation with children such that hope is not put on a timeline with behavioral objectives.

But sometimes, especially during busy times in kindergarten classrooms, although the face may be conspicuous, or maybe because children know the face is conspicuous, it can be a challenge to look into the face of a child. How can I see a child's face, when he will not even look at me? I remember worrying about achieving some instructional objectives with a child in my kindergarten class. I wondered how long I could justify my plan for this child's instruction to my administrator and the child's parents, when he seemed to be making little progress. I kept hoping that he would get it, hoping he would want badly enough to write that he would get over his fears, whatever they were. He avoided looking at me whenever he was approached with anything resembling print. Even his body turned away. Not only would he not look at me, he would not even cross over from the block area to where the tables were. He would not look at me even when I took a bin full of writing and cutting stuff to him. I could find no way to encourage him to interact with these materials or with me. It seemed that his hands were always full of blocks, his body in motion, his eyes elsewhere. As a last resort, I could have forced him to comply with my intentions, but I wanted to be sure that I had exhausted all other possibilities first. The very experienced classroom aide reassured me. "It's OK," she said. "Look at how he watches when I work with Sherry." She had seen what I had not. I reminded myself that we must watch so carefully, and not always where and when we think we should be watching! She was right. It was OK. Near the end of the school year, he was asking how to print Mom and Dad, and for help to write his name. He sat and listened to long stories if he had a lap to sit in. It was my own fear and pride that could have interfered with this child's attitude toward print. He became interested in print in time. It really wasn't too late for either of us. Sometimes I wonder what he might have thought about reading and writing if his first experiences had been forced, if his first experiences had not been with words that had meaning—Mom and Dad, and his own name. I like to think that he kept this self-motivated interest in learning to read and write. He moved at the end of the school term, and I never heard about him after that year.

There is something about face-to-face encounters, written by R. A. Cohen (1989), which seems to me to offer some insight into this dilemma that I encountered.

> The mushroom in the grass, the grass, the sky above, the stars beyond, do not make claims on me, nor question me, nor hold me to my place, vigilant, obligated, in the disturbing way that the face of the other does. . . . The concreteness and immediacy of the face—the alterity of the other person—plunges an exceptional hold or vigilance so deep into the self, endlessly, that the self is better than the ego, is more alert, more ready for the other. (p. 43)

Cohen writes about the mushroom, the grass, and the sky, when I might be thinking about the curriculum, but I think the comparison is useful. There is a difference between something outside myself, and the face. The face of another has a different hold on me. My ego is tied up in thought that is only thought. My own thought touches only me; there is no relation. However, the eyes in the face of a child not only touch but also hold me so that I have a sense of the child. I am then compelled to see the child's face in his body; a body clinging to blocks in a sea of classroom print! This child's hold on me is "ethical, the very orientation of myself toward the other person, myself beholden to" (Cohen, 1989, p. 43). Cohen reasons for the significance of the sensuous experience of the encounter with the other, particularly with the face of the other. We face the face of the child in situations that make ethical claims, disturbing and questioning us, compelling us to act.

PERSONAL KNOWING: MEANING BOUND TO THOUGHT THROUGH THE BODY

The process we have chosen to engage ourselves with has enabled us to begin to articulate the pattern that the teachers I have spoken to claim "is there somewhere." Our tacit, personal knowing is becoming visible. To extend Polanyi's (1958) analogy; our knowing, like sugar once dissolved in the tea, has become distilled, and lies crystallized in formalisms in the bottom of the cup. That is, the sense of pedagogical presence continues to shift form so that at least it can be grasped and seen as print.

We can say that our sense of pedagogical presence is a phenomenological remembering through our being. It is an experience of listening again and again to the stories of those who have been there before us, those who can laugh and cry with us. It is reaching out to touch beyond ourselves. It is the resounding resonance between us, the play of voices, the echo of laughter and tears. These are parts of the whole.

Our understandings thus far would suggest that these parts of the experience of pedagogical presence are recurring and embodied. We experience aspects of presence again and again, in shifting form but still of the same substance. The experience of pedagogical presence begins again and again as we return each fall, each term, each day, as my colleague says, "hoping, even though we should know better," laughing, and sometimes crying "What more do they want of me?" We cannot assume that one day we will know how to teach. We can only assume and hope that we may know a little differently, and thus, be better able to respond to the children.

The returning again and again is the path of our knowing. This is experience, not repetitive, not one year of experience repeated 12 times, but recurring, reverberating through our bodies. Our knowing is sensed, not in thought alone, but in embodied thought. It is somewhat like the child in my class who said one day after we had listened to part of Tchaikovsky's "1812 Overture," "That's how I feel when I'm waiting for my mom and she's not here." Our knowing is connected to our body-being-there. Our knowing reverberates through our body. Reverberation, Ricoeur (1991) suggests, is a phenomenon of

> echoing, *retentissement*, by which the schema in its turn produces images. . . . The effect of *retentissement*, reverberation or echo, is not a secondary phenomenon. . . . The ultimate role of the image is not only to diffuse meaning in the various sensorial fields but to suspend signification in the neutralized atmosphere. (p. 173)

Thus meaning is diffused in a myriad of possibilities, bound to thought through the body, searching for signification.

> Reflection [by itself] has no kind of primacy over the consciousness reflected-on. It is not reflection that reveals the consciousness reflected-on to itself. Quite the contrary, it is the non-reflective consciousness, which renders the reflection possible; there is a pre-reflective cogito, which is the condition of the Cartesian cogito. (Sartre, 1956, p. 13)

I am inclined to say, although it sounds strange, that thought, without body, cannot occur. Of course that goes without saying. Perhaps it sounds strange because we often forget that our thinking is bound to our bodies.

The problem we face as we attempt to understand this recursive reverberation between parts, as Levin (1985) suggests, is a problem of thinking. We are accustomed to a thinking that is separate from the gut-knowing that my colleagues spoke of. Levin advises us that

> We must let go, finally, of our metaphysical conception of thinking. We must simply *give* our thought *to* the body. We must take our thinking "down" into the body. We must learn to think *through* the body. We must learn to think *with* the body.

> For once we should *listen in silence* to our bodily felt experience. Thinking needs to learn by feeling, by just *being with* our bodily being. Are we ready to let this body of experience tell us how to think its "essence"? Are we as thinkers, ready to quiet the conceptualizing mind in order to *listen* to the body's own speech, its own *logos*? (p. 61)

Our bodies hold the meaning of our presence with the child, until, through the signification of music or language, or visual art, dance, or gesture, we make it visible. This is not to say that our minds do not also hold the meaning of our presence with the child; it is to say that our minds are necessarily an integral part of our body. We have for so long held the image of dualism in our thinking that we can no longer recognize the body's knowing. Levin's *inwrought thoughtfulness* expresses a quality that van Manen (1991) describes when he writes of thoughtful reflection.

> The significance that we attribute through thoughtful reflection to past experiences leaves a living memory that is no less embodied knowledge than are the physical skills and habits that we acquire in a less reflective manner. However, this thought-engaged body of knowledge of acting tactfully attaches a mindful, thinking quality to our ordinary awareness of our everyday actions and experiences. (p. 209)

Levin and van Manen suggest that to act tactfully is to claim our body knowledge, to live well focused in the body of those memories, to listen in silence to the language arising from our bodily felt experiences. The tactful act of teaching will be seen when we are pedagogically present. Thoughtful reflection will become *attached* to the ordinary awareness of our daily actions and experiences. Tact may become visible in the rhythmic movement of our memories, our listening, our acts of reaching out to the children, our voices, our silences, and our faces—through the time and spaces of our relations with children. To speak of presence differs from van Manen's talk of tact only in this respect, that tact is a way of telling, and presence is a way of being. To speak of tact offers a conception of pedagogical language through which we may hear the teacher's thoughtful voice and see the child who is interested, not "faking it," not cooperating "in a game of illusion" (van Manen, 1991, p. 196). To talk of presence offers a vision of the transformative qualities for our thought-engaged body acting tactfully within the ordinary awareness of our everyday actions and experiences. When you act in a tactful manner, that is, when tact manifests itself, there is pedagogical presence.

An example of this can be illustrated through a children's story that has been used in work with children who are experiencing life-threatening illnesses and medical treatments that are often associated with them. The book, *The Memory String*, was an impetus to begin using beads on a string to mark the passage of the children's treatments. In the hospital and clinic it is read to the children and their parents to express the significance of memories, of "true moments," and of being present with a child in a way that expresses a sense of reverence for the child's truth held in memories. The memory string is a string of buttons passed from great-grandmother to the child, Laura. A story was associated with each button, a first grown-up dress, an aunt's party dress, her mother's wedding dress, and one from the neck of Laura's mother's nightgown, the one she was wearing when she died. When the string breaks on the lawn, Laura's father and stepmother, Jane, helped to search for one last missing buttons until dark. Laura's father thought he could replace the missing button because it was one from his uniform; he could just cut off another and drop it in the grass for Laura to find. Jane said, "Laura would rather have that button missing than have a replacement. . . . It's like a mother, no substitute allowed" (Bunting, 2000, p.25). In the end, Laura's stepmother found the button and tactfully decided to leave it on the porch. "Like a gift from a good fairy" (p.28). Tact is manifested. Jane tactfully places the button on the porch and there, in this act, she expresses a sense of presence, a relation of being, showing reverence for another; expressed by the author as spirit (fairy). Lying in bed, Laura overheard the conversation through the open window, and the next day, noticing that the buttons on Jane's painting shirt were a pretty, deep, dark green, thought that maybe one day she would ask Jane for one to put on the string. Tact required presence.

Jane created a pedagogical space for Laura and for her father. She refused a replacement button. The pedagogical space that she created through her sense of presence is similar to that described by Parker Palmer (1998). He says that pedagogical spaces should be both bounded and open. "Space without boundaries is not space, it is chaotic void"

(p. 74). Spaces should be at the same time inviting as well as *"charged . . .* [students] need to feel the risks inherent in pursuing the deep things of the world or the soul" (p. 75). Both individual and group voices need to be invited. The "'little' stories of the individual and the 'big' stories of the disciplines and tradition" should be honored (p. 76). Solitude should be surrounded with the "resources of the community" (p. 76). "The space should welcome both silence and speech" (p. 77). In these ways, he claims that teachers make and hold connections in their hearts, meaning *"heart* in its ancient sense, as the place where intellect and emotion and spirit will converge in the human self" (p. 11).

To continue the search for an understanding of this organic relation will affirm the belief and confidence expressed by the teachers who took part in the research that contributed to the creation of this book. However, if we were to conclude this text here, with a listing of parts— remembering, hoping, reaching out, voice, silence, and face—we would be giving them up to exist as Sartre's (1992) *dead truths,* and thus they would be of little help to others, just another corpse of epistemology to add to Charles Taylor's (1991) list.

At the beginning of my questioning, one of the teachers who helped me to understand presence affirmed that there was a pattern somewhere. (She said this with more confidence than I felt at the moment.) My colleagues, who persisted in clarifying ideas and offering examples, knew this with enough certainty to continue with the question of pedagogical presence for more than a year. Thus, I came to believe that the search for a pattern was an ethical responsibility of my curiosity.

Again, therefore, it was necessary to return to the classroom to better understand the relationships between the parts that I my colleagues and I had discerned. I needed to watch and listen again, in order to discover how the parts could be made into a coherent whole that would be visible to ourselves and to others. Grace invited me to return to her first-grade class and Helen offered her combined kindergarten/first grade class. Together, they reassured me, we would be able to find a pattern. We were used to teaching children about patterns, and used to looking for patterns in children's behaviors and learning.

5

TEACHING WITH AN EMBODIED, AESTHETIC PERCEPTION

FRAMEWORKS AND FRAMING

My teaching colleagues speak of patterns, my academic colleagues speak of frameworks. I hesitate in conversations when the word *framework* is used. This is not a word that teachers use. They have not spoken of frameworks; instead, in order to create the text for this book, we have kept notes, we have scribbled diagrams, we have written in plan books, we have watched, asked questions and talked, then we have made more notes and diagrams—trying to make sense of our experiences. It seems impossible to fit the recurring and embodied qualities of our experiences within a framework. Framed and bound, our experiences would be confined within a static field. There would be no organic pattern, no flow, no river! To return to Levin (1985), who suggested that we must learn to think through the body, we find that it is an awareness of our senses that is a prompt to think through these senses, as if they are an inseparable part of the thought.

It is Suzanne Langer (1988) who reminds us that there is a branch of inquiry that long ago began as "an analysis of sensibility" (p. 49). It is an inquiry of the aesthetic. This word, *aesthetic*, is not part of our vocabulary. What does it mean? Almost 300 years ago Hegel (1993) claimed that if we were to understand the meaning of aesthetic perception "in its natural sense" we would know that it "means more precisely the science of sensation or feeling" (p. 3). The word itself has at different times been variously identified with one of three main ideas: the perceptual, the beautiful and the artistic. There is hardly anything of the first, the perceptual, surviving in contemporary usage, except in the negative form, "anaesthetic." . . . The term aesthetic was originally derived from the Greek work "aesthes" meaning to perceive (Diffey, 1995, p. 61–62).

To perceive is currently defined as meaning "to apprehend through the mind, . . . through one of the senses" (*Oxford Dictionary*, 1964, p. 819). If we interpret the meaning of *to perceive* to include all of the senses, and if we do not give primacy to the visual, we come "nearer to the language and sense of the ancients" (Kant, as cited in Diffey, 1995, p. 63). It is this interpretation of the original meaning of *aesthetic* that offers so many possibilities in the search for understanding the pattern of sensibility in pedagogical presence. Marcuse (1978) affirms this thinking when he suggests that to abandon the aesthetic form "may well provide the most immediate, most direct mirror of a society in which subjects and objects are shattered, atomized, robbed of their words and images" (p. 49). Thus, to adopt the aesthetic form as a perception of sensibility is to avoid the shattering and scattering of our experiences of listening, remembering, and hoping, of voice and silence, and of the face-to-face encounter into singular parts. We will begin with aesthetic form as it was understood so long ago.

RHYTHM: AN AESTHETIC FORM FOR THINKING ABOUT PRESENCE

"Rhythm—said Stephen—is the first formal esthetic relation of part to part in any esthetic whole" (Joyce, 1916/1964, p. 241). This reflection by Stephen, who is engaged in a discussion with his classmates on what beauty is, offers a beginning in the search for a pattern in the embodied sense of presence.

Sylvia Ashton-Warner who taught young children in New Zealand, offers another. Rhythm, she says, is the daily life of teaching and learn-ing. The day is a rhythmic pattern of breathing in and breathing out. The rhythmic pattern of in and out is her "organic" order. For example, in the morning the children are engaged in "conversation, crying, paint-ing, and quarrelling" (1963, p. 101). This is the time to "breathe out" (1963, p. 101). Later they ask for and are given assistance with reading, discussion, and stories. This is their time to "breathe in" (1963, p. 101).

Teachers of young children recognize this familiar pattern of children's days. When young children arrive at school, some are excited to see each other, some may miss their mother's goodbye hug and walk slowly around the room stiffly with head down to shield their tears from others' eyes, others may get their hands into centers such as the sand table—unless the teacher has put the lid on it. Even while completing the requisite attendance ritual, they are anxious to begin at their centers. Later there is a moment for the teacher to offer a story, a new song, to join a large group and work on a collaborative project. And then, there is a moment for running and yelling and building. In and out, in and out, until finally, they are at home, in bed, asleep.

Deleuze (1993) too claims the unifying power of rhythm. He offers a way to sense what

> is inadequate in its parts. What can be sensed may become sensible. Thus we may become aware of a vital power that overflows all domains and traverses them. This power is rhythm, which is deeper that all domains and traverses them. . . . This is the "logic of the senses" as Cezanne said, which is neither rational, nor cerebral. . . . It is diastole-systole: the world that captures me by closing in on me, the "ego" that opens to the world and opens the world to itself. (p. 192)

Rhythm is an experience of relation unrestricted by singular modes of knowing or expression. Rhythm is as Deleuze finds Cezanne saying, the "logic of the senses . . . a vital power that overflows all domains and traverses them" (1993, p. 192).

Thus we are offered a form, a dynamic and organic image through which we may conceptualize the relation of the resonating parts of pedagogical presence. Our conceptualization will be understood at the beginning to be a temporary structure, ready for the flux of experience, which is inevitable and necessary.

RHYTHM, ROUTINE, AND REPETITION: CIRCLE TIME

The image of rhythm in educational studies is not new, although it has not appeared frequently. The understanding we present is, in part, consistent with the work of Clandinin and Connelly (1986). They present an understanding of rhythm in which the concept of rhythm offers a possibility that "reconnects the practice and study of education more generally with the practice and study of living" (p. 386) and expresses a sense of coherence in school existence. However, the particulars we consider in this study are less focused on the curricular, calendar cycles, and more focused on the moment-by-moment intervals of pedagogical relationships. It is rhythm that sustains this moment-by-moment movement, which is the play (a to and fro) within the principle of reason.

An example of the moment-by-moment movement or the rhythm of relationships constituting pedagogical presence is described by Yeats in 1927. In his poem, *Among School Children*, he describes the to-and-fro movement of relations that he sees while inspecting primary schools in his position of senator. Yeats wants his reader to understand that we cannot separate one part of teaching and learning from another. As he walks through the classroom, he offers an organic image—a chestnut tree—and questions, "Are you the leaf, the blossom, or the bole?" (p. 1361), prompting the reader to reflect upon the futility of a search for a single, defining part of a dynamic organism. In the same way, he questions the purpose of searching for a single, defining aspect of teaching. "How can we know the dancer from the dance?" (p. 1361).

For Yeats, the labor of the classroom is a rhythmic movement of relation. We might interpret Yeats to be asking, "How could we possibly know the dancer from the dance, when one is the other as the blossom is the tree"? In a footnote to this poem, the editors of the anthology in which the poem appears comment that Yeats' view of life was as "a cosmic dance, in which every human faculty joins harmoniously. The individual becomes involved in the process, as the dancer becomes part of the dance" (pp. 1361–1362).

I believe that Yeats's dancer/dance in the schoolroom and Gadamer's image of dance[1] both offer a sense of rhythmic to-and-fro movement in the pedagogical relation between teacher and child. Play as "dance" and dancer/dance are reminders of the relational movement of differences within the whole.

RHYTHM: A LOGIC OF THE SENSES

Perhaps it is possible to understand the writing of Gadamer and Yeats through our own recollections, a phenomenological remembering through our being. Perhaps there was a moment when we questioned whether we were the leaf, blossom, or bole of the tree—some part. Or were we unable to distinguish our own self from the totality of the experience? For example, I recall learning something about rhythm and the dance while swimming in oceans. Late one summer afternoon I played with my children in the surf. Waves rose over our heads, sand and water swept over us. When I rested on the shore, and looked into the sunset, the waves reached up and out with pinkish, curling fingers. As they curled to catch us, these fingers poured sand. We laughed and swam and floated, beyond and on the crests of the waves. Sometimes we were swept along and rolled out onto the beach, to lie for a moment and watch those reaching fingers curl back empty-handed. I thought then that I knew waves. I thought that waves were always waves. But another summer, in another ocean, I found this was not so. I swam out beyond the breakers and lay in the reality of a word I had only known as a word—azure. So this is azure, I thought, and I swam in azure. It was not water in which I swam; it was a color, azure. I was reluctant to leave and return to shore; however, I knew I would need some strength to get in since I am not a particularly strong swimmer. I turned to the shore with energy to spare. But these waves were not letting me in, and I thought, "This is great. The French will think I'm some stupid Canadian who didn't have any sense about water." I thought about how we mock those who come to our country unprepared for the climate. I didn't want to be embarrassed, but neither did I want to drown! Young children were in this water, and they were able to get to shore, so there must be something about these waves that I didn't know. Then I realized that I was struggling against the waves. As soon as I stopped the struggle and swam instead with the rhythm of the waves—in with a wave, and out just a bit, gaining a little, holding a little, and giving a little, then in just a few moments I was tossed on the shingle. The next time was so simple.

I had learned something about the power of a rhythm that was not my own power, and something about the exhilaration of sensing and flowing with such a powerful force. I had thought I knew waves, but I had not. I understood now that the direction to the shore was not a straight line. It was a kind of magic to know the power of a rhythm that was not my own, yet was a power I could be with. There I was, *of one body with the river*, to use Hélène Cixous's words again.

The way to shore was not a two-dimensional path, but three or four. In a spiral, to and fro, within the waves' circular pattern of movement, I went out, swept almost to the bottom of the trough, and then back, carried up as the water surged forward again. Later, from shore I watched as bodies moved on waves, with waves, and beyond the waves to the shore. When the body is aware of the rhythm of the wave, even the children come to shore with ease. There are other ways to say this, and ways that come from the ideas of other cultures.

> The efficiency of *Wu Wei* is like that of water flowing over and around the rocks in its path—not the mechanical, straight-line approach that usually ends up short-circuiting natural laws, but one that evolves from an inner sensitivity to the natural rhythm of things. (Hoff, 1982, p. 68)

It may also be possible to understand rhythm as a logic of the senses through recollections of dance. I recall practicing for performances with a small dance company. Parts of dances, movements repeated—part by part, over and over, piece of music repeated over and over, part danced and danced and danced, stop and start—this is dance. But after all that, there comes the moment when the rhythm of the music carries the body and the body moves through the rhythm. The body moves on the flow of the music. Parts are indistinguishable, and the power of the one becomes the power of the other—and we do not want to know the dancer from the dance.

FROM ROUTINE TO RHYTHM

In the classroom we might experience rhythm through its absence, as well as its presence. One day, as I visited a friend's classroom on the day of the season's first snowfall, I began to question the difference between my experience of being in the children's morning circle when their teacher was there and when the student teacher was there.

Here, on this day, a student teacher was taking part in the routines of the classroom, just as I remember doing, imitating, watching, and trying to follow the routines of the cooperating teacher. As the children come in from their recess play in the newly fallen, wet, and sticky snow, and the student teacher asks the children to "Come and sit in a circle," it doesn't happen. The circle time does not begin well this day. The children are not getting to the carpet with ease. There are a few soggy mittens flying around in the air by the coats, scattering snow drops over heads, and as Grace enters the room, I can see that she is concerned. I have been watching, and now Grace and I help the children make the transition from soggy mittens to their classroom routine, showing the children with our expectations that they must respond to the authority of the student teacher in the same way that they respond to our authority. When the children are settled, Grace leaves to make a phone call to schedule a parent-teacher interview, and I suggest to the student teacher that I too will go off for a while. Grace and I want the children to know that the student teacher, Mrs. Marshall, can be responsible for them just as we can be. However, Mrs. Marshall responds to my suggestion that I too will leave, with laughter and says, "Oh sure! Go and leave me now!" So I too join the circle. Sitting in the circle with the children who are watching Mrs. Marshall show them how to create number sentences using a diagram of two hands on their math mats, and a tin of buttons, I am jostled by Sean who wiggles into my space and distracted by Jim who titters behind his hand, his eyes sparkling at a friend.

The children respond to Mrs. Marshall for a few minutes, and then they become distracted with each other, moving restlessly. Within milliseconds, I become the teacher, no longer observer or friend of their teacher. In my assumed role as teacher, I look at several children. It is the *teacher look*, an inclination of habit. The *look* is understood, and a few restless children withdraw into small movements of their hands, and focus on their crossed feet. They saw me look at them. Like Sartre (1956), grasping the "Other's look at the very center of my *act*," the children may feel "caught," now alienated from the freedom to plan possibilities for actions with their friends (pp. 353–354). It is not for me now to offer them other possibilities and the circle feels cut into pieces, disjointed and broken. I feel as though *the look*, like scissors, has snipped a connecting cord. What was the familiar classroom experience of being with children in a circle has become now unfamiliar. I have *looked* at several children, yet I cannot lead them out from their place of withdrawal. I would like to lead them out, along the line of my *look* to another point and other possibilities.

But this is not my circle and I do not enter the student teacher's dialogue with the children. Mrs. Marshall continues with the children. Those who withdrew remain concentrated within the space of their bodies, looking at their feet, at small movements of their hands. They do not look around; they do not watch Mrs. Marshall. I too withdraw, and begin to wonder about these spaces we create when we ask the children to sit with us in a circle. As Mrs. Marshall's questions and responses to the children crisscross this circle, my thoughts too crisscross time and space as I wander through memories and through the here and now of this moment. I recall and wonder about other experiences with circle times and gatherings together. I have not wondered about this before. The perplexity of that moment clings in tangled confusion for days. How will I understand this, our confusion? We—the many teachers of young children that I have known—just always have a circle time. We have not done this from any articulated wisdom other than the shared experience of many teachers over a long time.

> From the wisdom of early childhood education, we know that circles build a sense of belonging, unity, and wholeness while providing an opportunity for self-expression and sensory integration. The positive value of circles has been well documented. . . . Look, listen, and use a "light" touch to uncover how to guide the process of their individual coping. (Cadiz, 1994, p. 84)

None of us had more answers than these. But we were used to this, and had various ways of coping—and none of these various ways included an immediate, anxious search for answers. We walk around and around the question, knowing that eventually we will learn the answer—and that in the meantime another confusion will develop. To run fast after the first would have us running in frenzied circles, and this we do not want.

Sylvia Ashton-Warner (1972) in *Spearpoint* offers some insight. She says, "For, contrary to what appears to be, routine has a rhythm and a rhyme to it which answers man's immortal need for monotony and symmetry, as well as for surprise" (p. 74). She connects routine and rhythm for us in this statement, as she does when she writes about the in-and-out rhythm of breath in the daily rhythm of the classroom. Thus she hints at a difference and a relationship between routine and rhythm. An awareness of rhythm, even though it may remain unvoiced, or tacit, is a logic of our senses that, like breath and the waves of the ocean, sustains a rhythmic pattern of coming to know.

Like the circle in which the children are gathered, our experiences cycle through other days and again Grace sits in her chair and invites the children to "Make a semicircle. Sit down. We'll talk about our questions about mice." She gestures with her hands and smiles. She looks across the room where some children are still coloring at their tables. Now she is not smiling. They see her look at them with no smile. She pauses. They begin to put away the crayons, quietly chatting to each other. Grace continues with the children sitting. She stands up, picks up a felt pen, and asks, "What do we want to know?" The children who had been coloring come to sit in the clustered shape of the semicircle. Grace bends toward them. One of the children responds with, "What do they eat?" Grace reaches out to the children, sometimes with one step and sometimes three, to where they sit. Her arm moves into a child's space and back again. She moves, stepping and bending, reaching from child to paper. She writes the children's words on the paper, one color for the question "What do we want to know?" and another for the children's information. She steps again, down to the child with unclear speech, up with his words, repeating them with a grin, and a clear voice of congratulation for his information. She repeats his words and they are transformed into print.

With steps and turns, up and down, with half-turns from child to paper, she invites others to comment. With a one-step turn to a child, she invites him to offer his thought. She listens, close to his space. But now there is a pause. "No." Grace's head shakes the "no." Her palm faces him, the universal *stop*. He is going the wrong way. No, he must not say what the child before him said. He must not turn that into a "silly sentence." He must risk thinking for himself. She tells the child she will come back. He can have this space/time to search for his own thought.

PUTTING THE PIECES TOGETHER: THE
CHOREOGRAPHY OF A DANCE

And now we can begin to put together all those singular parts that we said were important aspects of pedagogical presence. Here is a touch that reaches out, a listening, the sound of voice, the feeling of hope, and the look in a face. Another way to talk about the sense of pedagogical presence is to say that it is *a reaching out to touch, a resounding resonance between us*—the play of voices, the echo of laughter and tears.

Reaching, back and forth, moving into and out of the child's space, Grace's actions invite the child to move as she steps back. From thought, to words, to print, Grace's hand will carry the words across the space and on to be shared with the next child. But the children know they must risk, they too must make a move, and it must be their own move, they must make a step in this pedagogical dance. The teacher has called to the child. The child now must join. She has invited the children into this circle, drawn them into "a space where learners can fail, but not disastrously; space where they can venture up to and know their own local frontier of discovery, explore it and then return to the security of more familiar play or practice" (Hodgkin, 1985, p. 24).

One of the children who never before had said more than two words together, even last year when Grace taught him, takes the risk today. Today he speaks two sentences. He is a small child and his voice is small. Grace steps forward and down, close to his face, and smiles.

Later she sits and asks me with breathless excitement, "Did you hear Charles? Did you hear he said two whole sentences?" I listened, waiting. With such breathless enthusiasm, more was sure to follow. And more did follow. In the year and a half since Charles had left the refugee camp to come to Canada, he had never spoken more than three words. Grace had taught him since he came to Canada. This was the most that she had heard him speak in English. Pedagogical presence is listening, with a silent understanding, to the meaning outside the words.

Day after day, the experience of watching/listening, and responding, watching/listening, and responding, again and again, acquires a familiar, rhythmic pattern until it is no longer thought about. Within the rhythm of this routine, the teacher could focus on a child's hesitation, a child and his newly found expressions, another child and that child's love of conversation. Within the rhythm of the routine, when Charles responded as he did, then Grace *knew*, with breathless excitement, that she had been learning to act with the right responses. She was learning some right steps in the move toward teaching Charles to engage in conversation in English and to engage in an inquiry process of thinking.

On another day, in another space, with other children, I watch in Helen's kindergarten/first-grade class. I watch as she too invites the children into the to-and-fro rhythm of her steps as they played with a new math program. Helen told me, as she brought out colored plastic cubes, the ones that make a sucking sound when you pull them apart, that she is "just learning how to use this curriculum." The portable, detachable, section of the program manual was within reach on a shelf, just in case she felt she needed to consult it. There was no need to leave the children's space and dash over to the desk to consult a hefty tome! She reached out her arm and with a sweep toward herself, as if gathering children; she invited several to join her. Together they showed others how to make patterns with five cubes of three different colors. With the children she chanted the patterns she made. "1, 1, 2, 2, 3, 3," and "a, a, b, b, a." The resonance of song/language gave voice to the visual, to the unseen thought.

Then she showed the children how to trick each other with expectations of pattern gone awry. She gave all the children cubes, and stepped back. We watched as, in pairs, the children took turns making a pattern with one mistake in it. Two children tricked each other with a twist of Helen's instructions. They made no mistake, and giggled while their partner looked for what they would not find. Helen joined the children in their laughter, in the double play of the trick, the surprise they crafted. She stood alone, then moved into the children's spaces, alternating moment by moment from the solitude of reflective watching, a surrounding of thoughts and memories, into the spaces where cubes make sucking sounds and children laugh as they discover the mistakes planned by their companions.

I laughed too when a child moved close to my ear to confide in me his crafty trick. Helen's eyes caught mine and, as if speaking for the children, she said, "These are some of the things Jane showed us this week." (Jane is a consultant who had been in the classroom with Helen, and the children and Jane had modeled her interpretation of the math program.) Today Helen could practice her steps in the new routine of this curriculum, as she took her turn to watch/listen and respond to the children. Their laughter and extended play with Helen's plan showed her this worked. She came to know more about children learning math.

Listening to the responses of the children, and watching them manipulate the materials, Helen came to know her instructional strategies were working. Sustained by a rhythmic returning to the watch/listen and respond, Helen connected a myriad strands of knowing into the steps of this dance and re-created curricular form. Permission, even encouragement to make mistakes, and to play with the idea of making mistakes, enabled the children to engage in a to and fro of exploration with the materials at hand.

The next time I visited, I joined the children near the back of their group on the floor, as Helen sat in one of the two green canvas director's chairs facing the children. I watched as the children watched Helen, waiting for the story. As Helen reached for the book, she watched several children who seemed to be inattentive and restless. This was not *the look*; the children did not meet Helen's gaze. She was simply observing. The children slid, inch-worming their way back on the slippery floor, toward the edge of the group, slowly coming closer to the shelf of cars and garages. Helen reminded them to stay in their own space, but this was effective only temporarily. I began to slide, inchworm-like, toward these children. Helen watched the children, she listened, our eyes met and she continued to read a few more sentences of the story. Then she paused, and invited the two children to sit closer to her. "Come and sit over here," she smiled and gestured to the floor by her feet. I wondered if they would change their pattern of movement. Helen watched/listened/and watched again, as she continued reading the story. The two children slid closer and closer to Helen and the book. Slowly they raised themselves higher, closer to the book, smoothly sliding around and up—right beside Helen, their eyes fixed on the pages of the book. They slid upward, unfolding their limbs until they were standing at her elbow, their heads hovering over the pages so that they were sometimes blocking her view of the words. Helen shrugged her arm and shoulder, and so created a space in which she could see the words. She invited the children to stand behind her elbow. They moved behind and hung their heads over her shoulder. Helen showed me again, as Grace had, that teachers listen, with a silent understanding, *to the meaning outside the words.*

This is the choreography of the dance. The teacher has invited children into a space created for them, close to the book and close to her. This is how they know to use this space. This is what they know of an adult's invitation to read with them. Helen has learned, she says, that some of the children are still lap-readers. Their parents extend invitations to read with them, touching, sharing the intimacy of telling stories. This is an expression of what they already know of the invitation to read. Their teacher knows the closeness these children associate with the reading of stories—the children breathe within her space, and lean into her body. Helen showed me how teachers reach out to touch through the space created with their being.

Helen and the children have choreographed a pattern of steps with the alternating rhythm of "familiar/unfamiliar/familiar," an invitation, reaching out through risk. She has invited the children to share her space. She extends one hand to help the child climb into her lap, and she supports another child's arm with her back. The children know the steps of invitation and intimacy. Helen has watched and listened to see what the children know of reading. Now, in the classroom, while reading to the group, Helen extends an invitation to the children to step into a cyclical dance of relation. She has helped the children to make a connection between their experiences at home, snuggled with their parent in the intimacy of the reading relationship, and the reading relationship within a larger group.

Eventually she would like to help two of the children take the risk to extend themselves further into the unfamiliar, into that space in front of her, where the other children sit now, watching and listening to the story from a distance. She does not yet know just how she will do that, any more than she knew just how the children would respond to what they call a chapter book. However, not knowing becomes an impetus to continue the steps of this cyclical dance: watch/question, listen, and reach out; watch/question, listen, and reach out.

Helen continues to "drift around on the edge of their thinking" (Paley, 1986, p. 131) searching for a place to land, if only momentarily. Not knowing, we search within the rhythm of this watch/listen, respond cycle. "As we seek to learn more about a child, we demonstrate the acts of observing, listening, questioning, and wondering" (Paley, 1986, p. 127). We sometimes land in moments so small that they are almost unnoticeable—a glance at one child, a shrug to make room, a teacher's arm surrounds a child who leans into her shoulder, a teacher bends down toward a child, steps back and up, carrying child's thought to transformation on paper. We repeat these steps again and again and again. Through these shifts of time and spaces we are looking to see what the child does not say. We begin to know that some children need more time and encouragement as we insist that they risk expressing their own thoughts. We learn that "Some of the kids are lap-readers, wanting to be read to the way they are used to at home," says Helen, whose lap is being sat upon. Thus we are better prepared to take the next steps.

We step as if our teaching practice were a dance. The image of dance enables us to conceptualize our stepping as an act of moving toward a knowing wrought through heart and gut. "That bodily felt quality of inwrought thoughtfulness," which is what Levin (1985, p. 296) names dance, is the pattern of our pedagogical relation with the children.

WE WILL NOT KNOW THE DANCER FROM THE DANCE

I have come to believe that the rhythmic pattern of steps that we take with the children resembles the steps of a dance rather than a linear march. It may be that the image of dance will suggest possibilities for conceptualizing. For example, we may conceptualize with the help of Levin's image of dance, and reason thus: if "Dance is the founding measure [beat or rhythm]" (Levin, 1985, p. 295), then a bodily felt quality of thoughtfulness is the founding measure of our knowing. Measure is not a static quantity in this conceptualization but rather is the tracing of a pattern of movement, of sound/voice/rhythm, known through the senses of the body. The dance cannot be without the dancer.

Thus the separation of object, self, and world (other) is no longer definite as we dance between, moving with the intention to seek steps that will guide us through our field of perception. Separation becomes a relation of teacher and children in a patterned movement of shifting, elusive boundaries.

Within the dance of this rhythmic relation of parts, the to and fro (Gadamer's notion of play) sustains continued questioning. As answers are found, questions arise, leading to more questions. Around and around, moment by moment, questions continually arise out of the context in which we found our answers.

It is this recursive, founding measure that enables a reflective sense of the "coherent existence" of our teaching practice, the "comprehensive entity" in which these particulars dwell (Polanyi, 1969, p. 125). The image of a rhythmic dance is an aesthetic form that safeguards the relation of part to whole. The whole is not shattered. Neither curriculum nor child nor teacher, not being or *technik*—none can claim primacy. All find place. Voice, face, touch, and silence, all move through the veil, which is the illusion of boundary between us. We look toward the particulars of one comprehensive entity—whether that is a curriculum guide, a program of studies, a child, or a class of children, and all the while we are aware that there is more.

Going 'round and 'round (trying not to be running in a frenzied circle) in our attempt to know what to do next, how best to respond to a child at one particular moment, we move "in an inevitable circle . . . that starts from the apprehension of indefinite-definite parts and proceeds to the attempt to grasp the meaning of the whole" (Pierce, as cited in Habermas, 1971, p. 170). This is the aesthetic of our perception. This is the analysis of our sensibility. One part of our understanding cannot exist without the other. A pattern of analysis and understanding cannot become known without the perception of the body's senses.

NOTE

1. At the end of chapter 3, I drew attention to Gadamer's notion of play as to-and-fro movement, which he suggests is an understanding of play that connects the object/subject. This understanding, he reminds us, "accords with the original meaning of the word spiel as 'dance'" (Gadamer, 1984, p. 93).

6

TEACHING AND LEARNING: AN AESTHETIC SENSE

MAKING MEANING OUT OF THE AESTHETIC SENSIBILITY WE CALL PEDAGOGICAL PRESENCE

The teachers who have contributed to this writing have shown us that our understanding of pedagogical presence with young children is an aesthetic experience of embodied, rhythmic relations, like that of the dancer and the dance. "At the still point . . . there the dance is" (Eliot, "Burnt Norton," 1961). And who would know the dancer from the dance? A vision of education that encompasses the technique and language of professional knowledge with the personal knowledge and language of the teacher/dancer, in an embodied and rhythmic relation with the children, requires, as Madeleine Grumet (1978) suggests,

> that we invest curriculum with the structure of experience that is aesthetic as well as technological. . . . I suggest that in this double vision will emerge a third form, the relation that exists between them, to be filled with human action. (Grumet, 1978, p. 279)

An aesthetic sense of pedagogical presence is an example of such a third form—an organic form that emerges through memories, voices, faces, filled with acts of reaching out to touch the other. As this third form emerges, it is important to notice that it is not static. "Neither arrest nor movement. And do not call it fixity" (Eliot, 1961, "Burnt Norton," line 64). Rhythm emerges from routine. A language of organic

metaphor and image emerges, conceived from a unity of differences, of
sense and senses. An aesthetic sensibility enables teachers to become
aware of the call to pedagogical possibilities. A teacher's perception of
surprise in classrooms acts paradoxically as a stopping (or arrest) of
thought and action, and at the same time, as an opening to pedagogical
possibilities. To be surprised is to experience a release into the unknown. Some may choose not to be released, not to explore in the space
of the unknown and may return to the familiar. However, for those who
choose to accept surprise, they may understand that

> Surprise, like blood, re-circulates through practic/se with the rhythm of para-
> dox. With the rhythm of the familiar/unfamiliar, the expected/unexpected,
> and the childlike/unchildlike holding child and teacher, surprise sustains
> the pedagogical relationship. (Hill, 1994, p. 350)

It may be that, in this moment, "the sensori-motor field is opened up,
and there is [es gibt] as space of enchantment" (Levin, 1985, p. 129).
And within that space of enchantment, we continue to learn to teach.
(Those are the good days, and I presume that we would not continue if
there were not many of those!)

The process of making meaning is as mysterious as the magical spells
of the fairy tales we read to the children. It is challenging to respond to
the differences and shifts in children's knowing, while being responsible
for the mandates of curriculum and managing the routines of day-to-
day life in the structures of schools. There are times when we feel that
we undergo transformations from frogs to princesses and princes and
back again as we attempt to respond to the multitude of variables in our
practice.

Anna's singing sound-sense, transforming voice to print, was an example of something that helped to clear a path for the journey. We learned
from Anna in her classroom that the rhythmic to-and-fro of "Sound-
sense, singsound, [and] bloodsong" is how we form the casts of meaning
for our teaching practice" (Cixous, 1991, p. 58).

> I have touched and been touched, listened and awakened only so much
> as I have experienced "the living creature that miraculously unites sense
> and the senses into one vox" and experienced the disturbance of that

form, playing with "articulations splitting up that body or reinscribing it within sequences it can no longer control." (Mallarmé, as cited in Caputo, 1987, p. 150)

As we live our days with the children and the curriculum, we shape the meaning of our pedagogical presence. We engage in a dynamic forming and re-forming of the senses, which reverberate through our bodies, awakening to learn and relearn, so that we are not one of the teachers who, after 12 years of teaching, really has only one year of experience repeated twelve times. Like Helen, we may carry a portion of a curriculum guide to the group of children. We may place it close at hand. We are aware that we would like to teach the children something about patterns this morning, but this is not the whole of our being with the children. If we are to reach them with the concepts of patterns in mathematics, we must reach out to them, quite literally, as Grace did, stepping to and from the children, carrying their words to be transformed from voice to print.

WHAT FORM DOES REFLECTION ASSUME?

The uniting of sense and senses, the re-forming of a curriculum that reverberates through mind/body of teacher and child in an ever-shifting form, is a phenomenon that continues to engage us. Even the shift of form that occurred as I created the text of this book intrigued my colleagues who were involved in its creation. In conversations about how we have tried to explain the process in this book, we came to a realization. It was Grace who said one day, "Do you realize we haven't used the word 'reflection' once?" The conversation stopped. She was right. My colleagues had never used the word *reflection* in any conversations. What then have we been doing if we did not talk of reflection in our practice and our understanding of pedagogical presence? Is reflection not one of the parts of pedagogical presence? What does it mean that we have not used this word?

I believe it means very simply that we have not used the word. The word—for some reason that we have not, so far, discussed—does not fit within the meaning of our experience. Whatever it is that might pass for reflection in our practice takes on a form not yet shaped through language. We have conversations with colleagues, or a moment's thought while standing between the playhouse and the blocks. We do not call this reflection. It is an awareness, the seeing of a flicker in an eye, a child's glance. We do not speak of reflecting. For example, was Helen reflecting when she spoke about providing opportunities for the children to have conversations? She did not use that word. She did not even describe the experience as thinking. She said that she had to *play* with the idea some more. "One of the things I'd like to create is the opportunity for them [the children] to talk. I don't even know what it would look like. . . . You have to *play* with it."

Helen's experience of reflection was a to and fro of watching/listening/responding, and thoughtful silences. Helen was engaged in a movement to and fro between the curriculum and the children. When Grace and her colleagues spoke about the two little girls who were plotting ways to stay indoors on a cold day, they were engaged in a to and fro of remembering and expecting, hoping and fearing, reflecting, as Schon (1987) might say, both in and on action.

Our experience of reflection is the embodied experience of relation with time and self and other. Sometimes we are not directed toward any goal, and therefore our reflection is playful in the sense that Gadamer speaks of play as a to-and-fro movement not tied to any goal. However, even when we are directed toward a goal, there is still room for play, as a colleague suggested when she said to me as Grace stood watching "Of course, Grace never got into any mischief!" Here is space for Grace to offer ideas about little girls who seemed innocent of any possible wrongdoing. Grace can, and does, respond in a playful way, acknowledging the recognition of shared knowing with a tilt of the head and a grin. She knows what this mischief might look like in the classrooms and hallways.

So—if all this reflection is happening, why have we not once used the word in our conversations? I believe it is because the image of reflection that is offered in education discourse is an image that emphasizes *technik* rather than that which is organic. For example, Schon (1991) speaks of a "Hall of Mirrors" (p. 355). The metaphoric value of mirror is helpful in coming to some understandings—for example, in the writings of Lacan (Grange, 1989)—but it is inappropriate for us in the classroom where reflection is an experience of embodied relation.

ANCIENT AND AESTHETIC
UNDERSTANDING OF REFLECTION

The difference between the metaphoric value of mirror and our understanding of reflection as an experience of embodied relation may help to understand the meaning of aesthetic form as it was at the time of Hegel. Almost 300 years ago Hegel claimed that if we were to understand the meaning of aesthetic perception "in its natural sense" we would know that it "means more precisely the science of sensation or feeling" (1993, p. 3). The very word itself has at different times

> been variously identified with one of three main ideas: the perceptual, the beautiful and the artistic. There is hardly anything of the first, the perceptual, surviving in contemporary usage, except in the negative form, "anaesthetic" . . . the term "aesthetic" was originally derived from the Greek word "aesthes" meaning "to perceive." (Diffey, 1995, p. 61–62)

To perceive is currently defined as meaning "to apprehend through the mind . . . through one of the senses" (*Oxford Dictionary*, 1964, p. 819).

Our sense and sense-making of classroom experiences, which is the "logic of the senses" that Cezanne talks about, is our return to aesthetic form (Deleuze, 1993). Langer (1988) reminds us that aesthetic form, as a branch of inquiry, began "as an analysis of sensibility" (p. 49).

We have listened to and followed the lead of the children into their worlds, where some mothers have parking meters beside their beds, where ice is melted cheese, and the playful music of pots and pans is the "death of harmony," where children tell us they "hear us with their hearts" and remind us in their drawings that the "sun is allowed everywhere" (Hill, 1994, pp. 340, 344). In the search for a language of the classroom, we have discovered an aesthetic form through which to conceptualize pedagogical presence. We have learned to hear with our hearts, embodied in the time/space of a child's presence (Hill, 1994). We have discovered the "power of aesthetic form to call fate by its name, to demystify force" (Marcuse, 1978, p. 51). And the force that we have sought to demystify is the day-to-day relation of being in the classroom with the children, teaching and learning. It is this aesthetic form that is our reflection. As Helen showed us, we call it *play* with thinking!

The power of aesthetic form has been lost to us for a very long time. It has been lost to us for so long that its recovery requires explanation. I would like to explain this by recalling a myth, Ovid's story of Narcissus at the pool.

Ovid says that Narcissus looked into a pool of water and fell in love with the image he saw. When Narcissus reached out to touch the image, he first thought he was reaching out to another person. However, in the act of reaching out he realized that it was himself he wanted to possess. "The image is my own" (Ovid, trans. 1986, line 464). Later in the poem, Ovid tells us that as Narcissus's tears rippled the darkening water, "The troubled water veiled the fading form" (line 488).

Just as we would, looking into a mirror, Narcissus sees himself reflected in the still water. However, Ovid tells us that the water is disturbed by Narcissus's tears, and the elusive image fades. A mirror will not be disturbed, it does not respond with ripples to my tears. My image does not fade when I look into a mirror; I cannot respond to warmth or bone-aching cold when I touch a mirror.

What is the understanding that Ovid intends in this telling? How does Ovid's understanding differ from the understanding of reflection conceptualized through the metaphor of mirror that has dominated our academic discourse? What power is here that will help us to demystify our relation of being in the classroom?

Ovid's tale of reflection is an organic tale. I believe he is suggesting that reflection is an act of reciprocal relation. It is when we fail to understand the nature of our reflection that we place ourselves at risk—as Narcissus did. When we cannot understand our self in relation with other, we endanger the life of the self. Narcissus can only wish that his love for himself would not be so intense. He cries out, saying "I could wish my love were not so near!" (Ovid, trans. 1986, line 469). He does not see himself in relation with another, only in relation with himself. He is a self-absorbed being and "So by love wasted slowly he dissolves" (Ovid, trans. 1986, line 492).

We have replaced the organic and dynamic image of our mythology with the *technik* of the reflective mirror, and we have lost the understanding that reflection is an act of being, a reciprocal relation of life. The teachers who have contributed to this book have articulated a look into something other than a mirror. These teachers and I believe that the experience of reflection is entwined with the experience of coming face to face with a child, reaching, listening, and remembering. Reflection reverberates through our mind/body, and finds expression through the aesthetic form in the rhythmic dance of relation described so long ago by Yeats.

LET GO OF THE MIRROR METAPHOR

Mary Rose O'Reilley (1998), in a chapter enticingly titled *Listening Like a Cow*, tells us that "We have to be conscious about the metaphors we choose to describe our relationship to students and resist those thrust upon us by the marketplace" (p. 23). I would suggest that it is helpful to let go of the mirror metaphor, to get out of the boat that it is, and get into the river. There, in the river with the children, the rhythmic pattern of an organic movement forms and traces the dwelling-in of our encounter with curriculum, self, and child(ren). It is there in our *dwelling-in place*, as Polanyi (1958), refers to our contextual and personal knowledge, that we find living form for our reflection. Reflection reverberates through our mind/body when we look into the face of a child and see by the spark of her eyes that we are understood. When the child crawls up the arm of the chair to sit on our lap, we shift our bodies and the book to accommodate the child's body.

Contrary to what Russell and Munby (1991) suggest, there is no framing or reframing in our experience of reflection. We face the child, but the child also faces us, we touch the child as he or she sits in our lap, and we are touched by the child. The boundaries of our relations are not definite. Where would the frame begin and where end? And would the frame serve to contain the image? And what value would there be in containing the image?

WHAT NOW?

We shall not cease from exploration.

—Eliot, 1962, p.1500

I have borrowed word forms and patterns from Eliot throughout this book. Again, I borrow from him to introduce a paradox of time and experience. The end of our exploration, Eliot (1962) says, "will be to arrive where we started," venturing through an "unknown, remembered gate," knowing the place for the first time (p. 1500). These images from Eliot's poem "Little Gidding" introduce the paradox of the unknown, yet remembered. I may not know this particular situation, but there is something about it that is remembered. Through the unknown but remembered door, we have arrived where we started. Do we now know the place for the first time? How much of our teaching is like that?

We bring our memories to teaching and learning, felt within our bodies. If we do not acknowledge the sense of memories past and the unknown possibilities of the future, then we will not know how to begin to look for the children. Stephanie says,

> We are so far removed from being able to empathize and to see the child as a child. That has to come back. How often do we overlook, not see? Presence, that's what it is, you know. There are so many people who see no whole. When you departmentalize, you fragment, specialize, the same as medicine. Why can't we just specialize in children?

She means that to be present with the children, our pedagogical presence, we must understand *being* as whole—not fragmented.

Myer Horowitz, who was for a time president of the University of Alberta, took similar thoughts, in person, to every member of the provincial legislature during a time when early childhood education in Alberta was facing severe cutbacks. He quite literally walked his talk in an attempt to keep the child and adolescent as the focus. It is in their presence that our purpose is achieved. He said,

> Do you ever get the frightening feeling that we may have forgotten the child in all the discussion of programs and governance and the politics of education? . . . Always we must remember that our primary concern should be the education, development and welfare of children. . . . If we keep the child and adolescent as our focus in our deliberations, we shall achieve positive educational change in the 1990's and into the next decade, century and millennium—for we shall be dealing with education "beyond the bottom line." (1995, p. 8)

When we were his graduate students, Dr. Horowitz used to tell us about his early childhood in Montreal, and how his memories of those experiences shaped his thoughts about education. We must all remember that our own teaching in our classrooms and our thinking about this is for us too, an exploration of our beginnings. And, as Eliot (1961) says, we will not stop exploring. At the end, we will remember and we will know in a new way. In the presence of the children, you will learn how to teach every day and you will teach to learn every day.

Between two waves of being—that is where your senses take you if you are a teacher. You are present, in the still point between the waves of being, just as elusive and just as dynamic. To forget this is to forget our own childhood. To forget this is to put ourselves at risk of being unable to recognize the child. Stephanie claims that we must see the whole; we must know the whole so that we may know the child. Teachers claim that we must reach out to touch, we must see the child's face, and the child must know that we have seen. The teachers' claims are similar to Berman's (1989) claim described in chapter 2. Presence, he says, requires an awareness of a structure that complements the self/other, body/mind structure of thinking rather than the "self vs. other" (1989, p. 311). We are not engaged in an either/or issue. My idea is not better than your idea. Discourses must be inclusive, complementary.

The whole of our experiences; all our senses, must contribute to the meaning of education.

Philosophers, physicists, and mathematicians have been telling us for decades that we must acknowledge the whole/part relation. "The conception of knowledge through indwelling will help to forge the final link between science and the humanities" (Polanyi & Prosch, 1975, p. 37). It is in this manner that we will find the empowerment of our connectedness.

WHY IS IT USEFUL TO RETURN TO THE REMEMBERED GATE?

It is not difficult to remember once we are aware that remembering can be useful. As a graduate student I was once asked to write three stories of remembering. The stories had to be about whatever situations I considered to be educational. In this way, we would be able to have some text that would provide opportunities to discuss what makes a meaningful learning experience for children. Without understanding more than this, I began.

I remember the farmhouse yard, the tree-covered, page-wire fence where my great-grandfather's old green Cadillac had been parked for so long there were small trees growing inside it. I remember the same yard, but some years earlier. I am younger in this memory. Younger than I was when my cousins and I walked with fear and curiosity around the old car. I am so small now that, when crouched by a wooden crate filled with compartments of yellow fluff balls, the edge of the crate is up to my waist. I am watching my great-grandfather reach into the compartment with his fingers to nudge out a chick. My great-grandfather's huge, rough hands, so unlike my father's, gently nudge and lift the chicks one by one from their wooden crate into his grasp. He reaches to the dark doorway of the chicken coop, opens his hands, and each chick disappears into the darkness of the chicken coop. As I crouched by the box, he showed me how to do the same, and I imitated his gestures, watching as the chicks disappeared into the darkness of the chicken coop. I liked this man even though I had just met him. My mother said his name, "Grandpa," in a very special way. I had not heard her voice quite like that before. He showed me how to do what he could do—this big man with these huge hands knew what to do with these small, soft creatures, and he showed me. I don't remember that he said a word. I only remember that he showed me so carefully and was so gentle with these tiny creatures.

What did I learn about an educational experience in this act of recollection? It is possible to learn something without recalling a word that might have been said. Gestures convey profound meaning. Parents choose many teachers for their children—teachers who know that they teach through their silences and gestures; parents, who assume the power to choose many teachers for their children, have a powerful influence.

I remember again what it was to be with the child who played with experience of music and language, telling me of "The Death of Harmony." And now, here I am between the me who was and the me who is myself now. I am between the waves of then and now, of self and other, and of what was and will be. And, as always in schools, I am between the child and the curriculum.

In remembering there is a re-collection of what it was to be taught and to learn. Now it is possible to know what we had not known as children. Now we know what to look for. Now we know better!

PUBLIC AND PRIVATE LANGUAGES: UN-NAMING AND RENAMING "DAMNED THEORY"

Beginning the conversations about pedagogical presence again, and we are always beginning our teaching practice again, I would, as Hélène Cixous (1991) says,

> be wary of names; they are nothing but social tools, rigid concepts, little cages of meaning assigned, as you know, to keep us from getting mixed up with each other. . . . But, my friend, take the time to un-name yourself for a moment. (p. 49)

Be wary of names, and take a moment to un-name ourselves. We—my colleagues and I—have been wary of names, and have un-named our-

selves many times in our conversations. Naming and un-naming is a
process encouraged by children. Children who can organize and name
the *Death of Harmony* are children who think about language. At an
assembly in the gym, a principal told the children she was going to read
something to them from a book called *It Was on Fire When I Sat Down*.
A little redheaded boy in the kindergarten class seated on the floor in
the front row looked up, and said loudly enough for everyone to hear,
"Why did he sit down if it was on fire?" Adults may be fascinated with
metaphor and imagery, and children are as well, but often, as happened
here, they question the language we use. They remind us to do the
same.

In the company of children who persist in challenging us, the teachers engaging in the conversations about presence have connected with
theory and practice, with self and other (child teacher and even memories) in an interdisciplinary multiplicity of discourses. An interdisciplinary scholarship has enabled many voices to make what Cixous (1991)
called "soundsense," to move our thinking beyond the hegemony of the
discrete sense, such as the visual, or what Levin (1988) calls the "optical
paradigm," an "epidemic pathology" (p. 469).

Levin's epidemic pathology, which is pervasive throughout many discourses, has been named, in a moment of frustration, "damned theory"
by one of my colleagues. However, we must and do take the time to play
with the un-naming of "damned theory." The to and fro of naming and
un-naming engages us in creating meaning in the space between the
named (theory) and the known (practice). For example, on an occasion
when a few colleagues met together to attempt to connect the public
language of new directives from the district administration with their
daily practice, and their attention was not directed toward the person
giving the workshop, I lightheartedly asked those at my table, "Are you
present?" (I must have learned this from the children, perhaps from
the child who said to another, "You hoo! Are you there?") The person
presenting the workshop overheard the question, as teachers often
overhear their students' extraneous remarks, and responded with a dramatization of presence. *Presence*, this time was shown to us by the presenter of the workshop with what I would like to call a Grand Gesture.
With a ballroom stride, legs and arms reaching across a space with swift
grace, he was there beside our table. Someone suddenly said, "Ah ha,

proximity!" A flourish of arms completed the stride, and the turn of a head toward the audience (our fellow colleagues) was a grin, a knowing nod, eyes now turned toward the group of colleagues needing a teachers' presence. Laughter all around confirmed recognition of the act. We laughed knowing that presence meant more than proximity. Presence was dynamic, moving, swift, reaching across a room, a searching gaze with sparkling eyes and a smiling face looking for another face on which to land.

Perhaps there has been a little too much "Effectiveness Training" in our repertoire, and like actors on break, having played out that scene, we exaggerate and tease the role. With the public language of an effectiveness training program, the parts were isolated, labeled, and so *presence* became *proximity*—yet we knew that presence was more than proximity. Presence was shown to be a matter of listening, watching, of moving in and out, sometimes quickly, when observations reveal "something not quite right here." With a ballroom gesture our colleague affirmed the transcendent connection of movement/relation with language. Eyes, face, a gesture of reaching out, the laughter of voice—these signified the meaning. This is the private language of the pedagogical presence in which we dwell.

In this story, the private language of laughter was read by the presenter. The presenter and the teachers played with the nuances of meaning from private/personal and public codes. The ensuing interplay of meaning made sense as one language form was teased into another.

In her book *Teacher* (1963), Sylvia Ashton-Warner tells a story that I interpret as a cautionary tale about what happens when we cannot or do not share the public and private languages of teachers and children. In this story, a school was redesigned and rebuilt. Ashton-Warner tells about her first experience at the new school. Seeing the new school, she recalls a moment from a day spent in the old school. A child had come crying to her because his block castle had been broken. "That's why somebodies they broked my castle for notheen." She writes her unsaid response, "Nor all your tears wash out a word of it" (p. 224). Now, standing at the new school, she writes

> I look across the shining floor through the wall-length window, past the nearby walnut tree to the earth site of the prefab. It really is true that it

has gone. It's just absolutely not there. Yet that rocky, raftered little barn with its melting frost and its vociferous company has housed my own castle . . . that I had built as spontaneously as any of my Little Ones; block on block precariously, turret on turret dangerously, with archways, stairways and defending cannon . . . and now all I can see through this elegant modern window is an area of earth in the grass. . . . That's why somebodies they broked my castle for notheen; somebodies. . . .

Nor all your tears wash out a word of it. (p. 224)

All your tears will not undo what has been done by the builders. The castle of wood and frost, filled with the spontaneity of life, could not be found in glass and steel. The small bit of life remaining was framed and contained. Her image of a school was not the place of the builder. It seemed to her that this structure was not a place for children who created castles and cried tears.

Unless we are able to convey an understanding of what it is to be pedagogically present with young children, we will continue, like Ashton-Warner, to find ourselves and the children spending our days within instructional frameworks designed by the hegemony of *technik*: in metaphorical structures of glass and steel designed with transparent accountability and structural integrity. Not that there can be any argument against accountability or integrity of pedagogical structure. It is when the hegemony of *technik* becomes exclusionary and the frames of reference associated with it become the standard of discourse that difficulties arise. Exclusionary discourses cannot generate the range and complexity of ideas needed for the challenges of education today.

In *Releasing the Imagination* (2000), Maxine Greene expresses her concerns with the restoration of meaning in the language and images that influence the teaching and learning experiences of teachers and children in schools. She states that

in what Jurgen Habermas calls the "distortions" of context-free communication (1971, p. 164) in the language of costs and benefits, and in the language of instrumental reason by which phenomena are "explained," there exists among many purveyors of information a deceptive if not simply indecipherable reality of signs and symbols. The knowledge they present is not knowledge for its own sake, but it is secret knowledge nonetheless and often dangerous in its implications. (p. 46)

Even when knowledge is presented with the best of intentions, it is wise to listen with caution and to be aware of the implications inherent within metaphor and image. If we are aware, we may be more likely to, as Greene (2000) recommends, respond to the spaces where there are silences in discourse, "to link the secret places to public spaces," acting in support of Paolo Freire's ideals for transformative action (p. 48).

SUSTAINING A COMMUNITY OF EDUCATORS

My colleagues and I have generated an image of a spiraling, recursive, and reverberating logic of embodied knowing that enables access to an interplay of personal and professional knowledge, to past and present, tracing the pattern of this logic in a multidimensional pattern—a pattern that differs from the linear dialectic of theory/practice. We have opened metaphorical spaces for thinking and sharing what it is to be pedagogically present. It is to *be there*, aware, with *all* senses in play. *Presence* assumes an aesthetic form, an organic structure that encompasses both perceptual and intellectual sense.

We are now able to share what was previously an aspect of our tacit knowing, half-heard, in the stillness between forms of being (between the technique of curriculum guides, the children, and our colleagues). Grace says, "It's a relief. It's a relief to be able to talk with someone who understands early childhood philosophy. It gives us support between teachers. We've been trying to do this since we started teaching and now it's a relief." Another teacher explained that the time we have spent together in this writing has been an opportunity for her to develop a way to talk about

> the way we have always worked to connect what kids can do with the curriculum, as opposed to teachers like Joe and Susan who use a technical approach. Susan said to me before school started, "These are the *perfect* spelling books!" They were published in 1979! *Perfect*? They're more interested in the books than the kids.

This teacher had tried to show her colleagues the choices they had for new spelling texts, texts that were approved and recommended by the school boards. The old texts had been removed from the approved and recommended lists for school texts because they did not conform to current legislative guidelines for inclusive language and sensitivity to ethnic/minority populations. For her, and for other teachers whose parents were immigrants and survivors of the Second World War, issues such as inclusive language and sensitivity to differences were critical. What the children might be learning from the old texts might perpetuate attitudes that are no longer acceptable.

Sharing understandings enables teachers to reach out to each other through the boundaries that we perceive to delineate difference, and thus to change teaching practices, even if it is slow change. There is an interplay of language and aesthetic forms. The unfamiliar is recognized. As Stephanie said, laughing and looking at her language now distanced, at arm's length on the page, "Did I really say this, these words of wisdom?" She asks to take these words home; somehow they have changed form, being on paper and not in voice, and she tucks them away. Yes, these are her words. She tucks them away with a smile on her face. She recognizes them through their disguise of black ink on white spaces. They only appear to belong to me. I am the one who is simply their guardian for now, the one who has taken on the responsibility to share them in a public language. The words are returned to the speakers; they cannot withstand the strain of communicating without their connection to their creator. T. S. Eliot knew this. He knew that words on their own will perish and decay.

We continue with our questioning, within the places of our dwelling-in, and thus again we focus our energies on the teaching and learning of children. Perhaps in this way we will be better able to learn how to help children learn, and to understand how each fragment of the experience of being pedagogically present relates within the greater whole. Perhaps we will be better able to articulate this experience and thus to create a community in which we can support each other's learning.

We have formed the language of our inquiry through diverse public languages, such as conversations with children and colleagues, literature, and even parts of what one colleague named "damned theory." An awareness of diverse languages has made it possible for us to name and un-name, to re-form what was difficult to question, and to make presentable in the empirical and instrumentalist traditions of past decades.

We have perhaps found in this decade what others looked for when they wrote more than 35 years ago that

> researchers in education must never lose sight of this. All their quantifying, all their correlations, all their control groups, will add up to a sterile set of mulish charts if they ignore the role of the teacher. Teaching is nine parts art and one part routineness. . . . Nor will any dissertation ever discover the magic that makes Miss Blandish a delight to her students. Let us not reduce Miss Blandish to a standard deviation. . . . Let us kneel before the witchery of the good teacher as we would before Mozart. Let us not impale her on a specimen board and remove her wings. Let her soar. (Farrell, 1971/1996, p. 2)

We are no longer subject to a "tyranny of form" (Marcuse, 1978). The postmodern tradition of thought in many disciplines and logical structures has enabled diversity, thus we may learn, as Prigogine and Stengers point out, that

> No single theoretical language articulating the variables to which a well-defined value can be attributed can exhaust the physical content of a system. Various possible languages and points of view may be complementary. They all deal with the same reality, but it is impossible to reduce them to one single description. . . .
>
> The real lesson to be learned from the principal of complementarity . . . consists in emphasizing the wealth of reality which overflows any single language, any single logical structure. Each language can express only a part of reality. (Prigogine & Stengers, 1984, p. 225)

Complementarity recognizes no privilege of teacher voice over child voice, or theory voice over teacher voice. (Those who do not know what Prigogine and Stengers mean, those whose scholarship is exclusionary, will see their logical structure tossed from the experience of the child-teacher relationship—or they might find it on a shelf in a storage room.)

THE LANGUAGE WE CHOOSE TO USE FOR ORDINARY UNDERSTANDINGS

We are at a crossroads in our thinking in the Western world. Janus-faced, we look to the past and to the future, invoking old gods and the

new sciences. We must acknowledge the ambiguity of our humanity, our
"entre-deux" as Beauvoir (1947) describes it. Within this space of ambiguity, which is the context of our being, we may play! That is, we may
move to and fro between the multitudes of possibilities that surround
us.

An example of this *entre-deux* or connectedness is found in Prigogine
and Stengers's book, *La nouvelle alliance*. Immediately the title in
French conveys an image of connections, even for those who are not
familiar with the French language. *Alliance* in French and English have
similar meanings. I was disappointed to see that the English title was
changed to *Order Out of Chaos: Man's New Dialogue With Nature*.
This title suggests yet another dialectic, a repeat of the subject/object
separation of man and nature. I am disturbed with what seems to be an
introduction of dualities rather than an attempt to convey the original
title's meaning of a commitment to connect. Where is the whole, where
is the relation, the indicator of passion implicit in *alliance* in the English
title? Like the English dessert with the exotic name *blanc mange*, we
are deceived with language and served something bland and without
substance. Man and nature again are separate. Where is Cixous's relation of river and person? Is the implication that we must by all means
avoid the challenge of boulders that might have rocks and rivers? Where
is the thrill of reading the white water and negotiating the rapids?

The difference may be subtle, but I believe the translation carries a
message that suggests difference rather than relation. I would be more
inclined to accept a substitution in the wording or the title. If *dialogue*
were substituted with *play*, then at least Derrida's concept of a play of
differences, what he named *differánce*, could be encouraged. For example, Beauvoir (1947) claims that an ethic is associated with the realization that we live within the space-between-which-connects. Her
expression *entre-deux* is similar to Derrida's *differánce* "difference"—
both emphasize the to-and-fro between, rather than the boundary surrounding self. There is no wall. There is a semipermeable, organic
membrane, and thus we may touch and be touched by the other.

This shift in thinking, such as is described by Polanyi as well as Prigogine and Stengers, a shift that encouraged the search for connections
and relations would be consistent with thinking in disciplines other than

education (Berman, 1989; Levin, 1985, 1988; Merleau-Ponty, 1966, 1968; Nietzsche, 1969; Polanyi, 1958, 1966/1983, 1969).

When we are present, we live in a relation of memory, voice, face, touch, and silence, self and other. Our days are spent dwelling in a relation of encounter with other. To be pedagogically present is to dwell between these beginnings and endings of self and some one or some thing else. It is in the to-and-fro movement *between* this dwelling space of self and child that we experience pedagogical presence in the classroom. It is perhaps as Helen said it was: "More feeling than something you could describe. Peter said it was like walking into magic. Something that comes out of all you do. Finally all this stuff you've done, this little glimmer lets you know it's right."

To experience the death of harmony, and then smile, to learn to see a child skate on melted cheese, to move in a to-and-fro step with child, voice, and text as you transform voice to print, to shift your shoulder and create space for yourself and the child to see the book, to envelop a child who knows only the intimacy of lap reading—these are not straightforward tasks. These are the tasks of our everyday life in classrooms, our ordinary tasks.

It is essential, Greene (1988) advises, that we challenge claims to an epistemology of practice that does not respond to the "domains of ordinary understandings, . . . the language of daily life" (p. 54). She cautions educators that they must be aware of the relationships between the "demands of society and the requirements of human growth" (p. 53). Without this awareness, she suggests that our public space will be action "governed by technical rules based on empirical knowledge" (Habermas, as cited in Greene, 1988, p. 54).

CAN WE TEACH—CAN WE LEARN TO BE PEDAGOGICALLY PRESENT?

I have been asked, "Can you teach someone to be pedagogically present?" Years ago, in a seminar session at the Conference of the Canadian Society for Studies in Education (CSSE) in Montreal, I had a unique opportunity to discuss this question. One answer to this question emerged from the conversation that took place during and after the presentation. The context of this conversation is significant, and so I would like to describe it for you. As I walked down the hall to the room in which the seminar was to be held, it occurred to me that nothing in the program indicated whether this presentation would be offered in English or French, and since this was Montreal, an assumption could be made either way. I walked through the door of the classroom and immediately was asked, in French, whether the presentation would be done in French. I responded in French that since I wrote in English, I would prefer English, but I would be happy to answer any questions and to discuss the paper in French. The response was offered in French, that this would be OK, since I seemed to understand. I did not at first know what was meant by this response. What did he mean, *understand*? I knew the words, but once again, I asked myself, what is the meaning outside the words? The issue of language was a priority. This would be a group that was already aware of the *sense* of language and meaning. It was not until later in the dialogue that I understood the implications of this awareness.

The group of approximately 15 was composed of people from a variety of linguistic and cultural backgrounds; Francophone, Anglophone, Arabic, and Muslim. Most were educators of teachers; some were teachers. During the presentation and following, they related several anecdotes that clarified not only a response to the question of teaching pedagogical presence but the notion of asking the question itself. Thus the dialogue offered an opportunity to answer the question through a return to the question itself. Can we teach someone to be pedagogically present when this requires an awareness of embodied being, of which language is one aspect? One of the teacher-educators told of his experiences as someone from an Arab culture attempting to understand both the language and the gesture of a conversation. In the Arab culture, "no," he told us, is signified with a nod of the head. He was aware that in Western culture, a nod signifies "yes." Thus, he explained, when the meaning of a conversation is ambiguous, the gestures may be critical and we must attend to all aspects of language if we are to convey meaning when we are with our students, no matter their age. This was, for him, one reason to be discussing the meaning and significance of pedagogical presence. Another teacher-educator commented that in our schools the same situations exist and it is this knowledge, and these skills of awareness, for which we are preparing student teachers.

We began to understand that we were all talking about a willingness to be open, that is, to watch and listen, and to question without making judgments, accepting and responding to each other's communicative intent. Not to do so could lead us into moments of embarrassment, confusion, self-doubt, anger, and unwillingness to continue. Thus the answer to the question of whether or not we can teach someone to be pedagogically present became the shared understanding that *we have no choice but to be pedagogically present* with all of our senses if we are to hear and understand each other. We must not only be pedagogically present with the children, but with each other as well. The differences among us are such that similarity of language is insufficient for understanding. Language is gesture as well as word—and a nod may not always mean "yes"; thus, we must see the face, and look for the gesture. We can only do this through an awareness of our encounter in the presence of the other.

Can we teach student teachers to be pedagogically present? Is the answer to that question not already made implicit through the establishment and continuation of practicum programs? Have we not assumed that student teachers can learn to be pedagogically present, and that one significant condition for this learning is that they be in the child's space, in schools?

I asked Grace what she thought.

> Many student teachers are capable of being this way immediately, but many are too scared. The last one I had was a mom with an 18-year-old handicapped child. She could teach and discuss like we do. And she's had two job offers. She's a confident lady who knew what she was getting into. Whereas another student teacher was too immature. She didn't have the experiences. Mind you I've had older adults who should've had experiences and they haven't been able to be this way.

When we begin as student teachers, we may simply stand looking, without the insider appreciation for seven-year-olds and their knock-knock jokes, without an awareness of the steps necessary to transform routine into a rhythm of relation. Perhaps when we begin, we are aware of the "unmanageable ambiguity of background commonsense" (Varela, Thompson, & Rosch, 1991, p. 148). We may have a beginning of that knowledge, in the form of awareness or remembering, and feel overwhelmed and confused. We know when something is not as it ought to be. We know when we are missing something even though we may not be able to name it. It is the knowledge of how to transform this awareness that is one of the challenges in the classroom.

Yet, this is a beginning, "in fact, the very essence of creative cognition" (Varela et al., 1991, p. 148). Here is the space/time for the development of what Habermas (1971) describes as practical wisdom. Beginning with the "presupposition of practice, we call the knowledge constitutive interest . . . [we aim] not at the comprehension of an objectified reality but at the maintenance of the intersubjectivity of mutual understanding, within whose horizon reality can first appear as something" (p. 176). Talking and acting together, action and conversation, he claims, help to generate a "practical wisdom" (p. 177). I remember again what Stephanie said. It is worth repeating.

> You have a choice. You want to or you don't. It depends on how deeply inquisitive you are, if you are curious to see. Some people have the expectation of children to be so adult-like. When they behave so child-like, not like small adults, people don't want to see them. [She laughed.] It's not always so good to be an adult!

Because diversity creates the necessity and the opportunity for learning to be pedagogically present, perhaps we should not be asking whether or not we are able to teach student teachers to be pedagogically present. Perhaps we should be asking *who* is the *we*, and *how* we can teach. Will *we* be teachers and school staffs as well as universities and university staffs? Will we work collaboratively? Will universities cut back and cut back on their involvement with schools, believing and/or hoping that teachers and student teachers will be able to create environments that support learning rather than opportunities to relieve teachers of increasing demands by tapping into a very cheap source of temporary labor? Will we support collaborative efforts to nurture student teachers with connections to schools from the time they enter university? Again, is there a common understanding of who the *we* is?

In what variety of ways can student teachers be provided with opportunities to be pedagogically present? How can student teachers be pedagogically supported, guided through opportunities to be pedagogically present with young children of diverse backgrounds and abilities? How many opportunities can be created to engage in dialogue with student teachers so that they are enabled to question and to return to the question, to learn to expect no closure and no certainty, to always remain engaged in the process with supportive colleagues?

CONCLUSION: FUNDAMENTAL PRINCIPLES

We Have an Obligation to Be Real

I believe it is through pedagogical presence, dwelling with the child, that we become *real* teachers. Perhaps a children's story, *The Velveteen Rabbit*, helps explain what I mean.

> "When a child loves you for a long, long time, not just to play with, but REALLY loves you, then you become Real."
> "Does it hurt?" asked the rabbit.
> "Sometimes," said the Skin Horse, for he was always truthful. "When you are Real you don't mind being hurt."
> "Does it happen all at once, like being wound up," he asked," or bit by bit?"
> "It doesn't happen all at once," said the Skin Horse. "You become. It takes a long time. That's why it doesn't happen to people who break easily, or have sharp edges, or who have to be carefully kept. Generally, by the time you are Real, most of your hair has been loved off, and your eyes drop out and you get loose in the joints and very shabby. . . . It lasts forever. (Williams, 1983, pp. 4–5)

It would seem that through living in relation with an *other*, the object (toy) ceases to be objective (a toy), and in its place comes into being something different, a little Rabbit, pregnantly alive with possibilities.

> Later, left outside the garden shed to be burned with the other toys gathered up by the nanny, the rabbit shivers tearfully.
> And then a strange thing happened. For where the tear had fallen a

flower grew out of the ground, a mysterious flower, not at all like any that grew in the garden. It had slender green leaves the colour of emeralds, and in the centre of the leaves a blossom like a golden cup. It was so beautiful that the little Rabbit forgot to cry, and just lay there watching it. And presently the blossom opened, and out of it stepped a fairy. (p. 23) . . . And she came close to the little Rabbit and gathered him up in her arms and kissed him on his velveteen nose that was all damp from crying. . . . "Now you shall be Real to everyone." And she held the little Rabbit close in her arms and flew with him into the wood. (Williams, 1983, p. 26)

To dwell in relation with another may bring tears, as the Velveteen Rabbit learned. To dwell in relation, dwelling-in the world, is to cry and to forget to cry. To live in relation, to indwell, is to become Real.

We have returned from that journey we set out upon, through the Janus-faced gates of this century's postmodern knowledge structure. We have returned to arrive at what we have been trying to do since we started teaching, and are relieved to know the familiar for the first time.

The ethic of questioning prompted a beginning, and the ethic of play sustained the moves through a play of methodologies. It was, as I imagine Caputo might say, a "play of difference [that] is not oppositional difference, but let us say, differential difference, the pure play of multiplicity, becoming, and chance" (1993, p. 47).

An ethic that recognizes this play of difference has been critical. This play of differences "open[s] up ethics to the inevitable difficulties of life" (Carson, 1996, p. 18). "Difficulties are to be expected," my colleague says. Thus we understand ethics not as an ethic that begins with a capital "E" and thus removes itself from the ordinary, saying "Notice me, I am something special." Ours is an ethic of ordinary life, the kind we recognize each morning as we enter the school and encounter the children. Because I am with the child, as teacher, I am "obligated," Caputo (1993) would say, to respond within the horizon of the child's experience. "Obligations happen for the while they happen and then fade away. That is all there is to them. But that is enough. They do not need to last forever" (p. 237).

The teachers who participated in this research have chosen to be obligated. Helen says, "If we believe it is important to be present with the children in these ways, then we structure our schedule in certain ways."

Not all teachers believe this is important, and not all teachers choose an ethic of being with children, although they are in schools with children. Some teachers choose to look over the heads of the children who are attempting to talk with them, some choose to teach from books that hold no interest for the children, whose pedagogical value has been determined inadequate by the boards that employ the teachers.

To and fro, in each encounter with an other, we have articulated that which becomes visible through the hermeneutic process, the biographical remembering, and the act of reaching to connect. As one meaning elicits another, the biographical, the phenomenological lived experience, and the hermeneutic are transformed and transformed again.

Our Language Must Include Organic Metaphors

A language that includes organic metaphors reverberates through bodies and time. It is an expression of the rhythmic logic of our body's inwrought thoughtfulness, that which enables children and teachers to sustain a pedagogical relationship. This language form may enable teachers to make visible what we know, and to share this with student teachers, with parents, and with the communities in which we live and work.

We Must Understand Reflection as an Organic Act of Reciprocal Relation

It is important for us to recover Ovid's ancient understanding of reflection as an organic act of reciprocal relation. Through that image of reflection, we may understand the emergence of a third re-forming of our teaching practice—neither aesthetic nor technological, neither child centered nor curriculum based—is a form of practice that emerges out of relationship.

We Must Make Connections Through Diverse Traditions and Cultures

Our questioning about pedagogical presence has left untouched vast realms of literature, both oral and written, which relate to the question of presence. For example, we might investigate aspects of Western philosophy that explore the concepts of chaos[1] and self-in-relation. This may help to further open our thinking and to develop a language through which we might articulate what is unique about teaching and children learning. It would be helpful to be able to speak of teaching and learning without stumbling over meanings derived from languages intended to speak of medicine or anthropology or the social sciences.

> In our age, in which the true meaning of every word is encompassed by delusion and falsehood, and the original intentions of the human glance is stifled by tenacious mistrust, it is of decisive importance to find again the genuineness of speech and existence as We. . . . Man will not persist in existence if he does not learn anew to persist in it as a genuine We. (Buber, 1988, p. 98)

We can learn from the languages of other cultures. There are other cultures for which understandings of the *we* is explicit and implicit within their language. An understanding of existence as *We*, for example, is contained in the Thai language. In Thai, there is no word that can mean *I* by myself. There is only *I* in relation to my parents, my job supervisor, my spouse, my child. Each *I* is a different expression of relation.

The intention will be to understand a third form of existence, not me or you, but *between us, in relation*, which is the essence of pedagogical presence. Or, as Maxine Greene (1995) has said more recently,

> Our presentness to ourselves depends to a large degree upon our capacity to remain in touch with the perceived world in its completeness and openness, to *think* that world while also keeping our consciousness open to the common culture our ideas cannot but express. (p. 53)

With others, she challenges us to concern ourselves with understanding and making decisions according to our own responsibility, to recognize false consciousness, and to live as an embodied consciousness.

To live in this way in the classroom is to understand what Aoki (1993) said about life in the classroom, that it is "lived in the spaces between and among . . . where something different can happen or be created" (p. 69). We must be prepared to see, to hear, to listen, to speak, to touch and be touched, to know the empty, open spaces. We cannot do so with our heads alone; we must be embodied, present with all of our senses. We must come with, and to, our senses. Perhaps in these ways, we will become *real* teachers.

A LETTER TO THE READER

This letter below was written by a child in kindergarten at the end of a school year. The spelling has been corrected to make it easier for adults to read.

Goodbye
   I hope you have a good time with the other children next year and I will miss you very much. I promise that you will be in the middle of my heart for sure so that means I love you.

And, for sure, we will return to a beginning again in the new school year. We will return with memories held in our hearts. So I want you, the reader, to remember: "Knowledge of the object, impossible without idealization, is merely the freezing of an existential state. It puts an end to the personal plenitude achieved in the encounter, in relationship, in the covenant between single ones" (Buber, 1988, p. xiii).
   Now, return to the children, and be present with them again.

NOTE

   1. "Chaos, *khaos*, *khaino*, means 'to yawn'; it signifies something that opens wide or gapes. We conceive of *khaos* in most intimate connection with an original interpretation of the essence of *aletheia* as the self-opening abyss (cf. Hesiod, *Theogony*)" (Heidegger, as cited in Levin, 1998).

REFERENCES

Altrichter, H., Posch, P., & Somekh, B. (1993). *Teachers investigate their work: An introduction to the methods of action research*. London: Routledge.

Aoki, T. (1993). Contestaire: Themes of teaching curriculum. In T. Aoki (Ed.), *The call of teaching* (pp. 111–114). Vancouver, BC: British Columbia Teachers' Federation Program for Quality Teaching.

Arendt, H. (1978). *The life of the mind*. New York: Harcourt Brace Jovanovich.

Ashton-Warner, S. (1963). *Teacher*. New York: Simon & Schuster.

Ashton-Warner, S. (1972). *Spearpoint*. New York: Alfred A. Knopf.

Barthes, R. (1985). *The responsibility of form*. Berkeley: University of California Press.

Bateson, G. (1979). *Mind and nature: A necessary unity*. New York: Bantam Books.

Berman, M. (1989). *Coming to our senses*. New York: Bantam Books.

Beauvoir, S. (1947). *Pour une morale de l'ambiguite* [The ethics of ambiguity] (15th ed.). Paris: Gallimard.

Buber, M. (1988). *The knowledge of man* (M. Friedman, Ed.; M. Friedman & R. G. Smith, Trans.). Atlantic Highlands, NJ: Humanities Press International.

Bunting, E. (2000). *The memory string* (Ted Rand, Illus.). New York: Houghton Mifflin.

Cadiz, S. (1994). Striving for mental health in the early childhood centre setting. *Young Children, 49*(3), 84–86.

Carse, J. (1986). *Finite and infinite games*. New York: Free Press.

Caputo, J. (1987). *Radical hermeneutics: Repetition, deconstruction, and the hermeneutic project*. Bloomington: Indiana University Press.

Caputo, J. (1993). *Against ethics: Contributions to a poetics of obligation with constant reference to deconstruction*. Bloomington: Indiana University Press.

Carson, T. (1996). Not ethics but obligation: Confronting the crisis of relation-
    ship in collaborative work. *Salt: Journal of Religious and Moral Education
    Council, 17*(1), 13–18. Edmonton: Alberta Teachers' Association.
Cixous, H. (1991). *"Coming to writing" and other essays.* (S. Suleimen, Ed.;
    S. Cornell, D. Jenson, A. Liddle, & S. Sellers, Trans.). Cambridge, MA: Har-
    vard University Press.
Clandinin, D. J., & Connelly, F. M. (1986). Rhythms in teaching: The narrative
    study of teachers' personal practical knowledge of classrooms. *Teacher &
    Teacher Education, 2*(4), 377–387.
Clandinin, D. J., & Connelly, F. M. (1991). Teacher as curriculum maker. In
    P. Jackson (Ed.), *Handbook of research on curriculum: A project of the
    American Educational Research Association* (pp. 363–399). New York: Max-
    well Macmillan.
Cohen, L. (1993). *Stranger music.* New York: Pantheon.
Cohen, R. A. (1989). Absolute positivity and ultrapositivity: Husserl and Levi-
    nas. In A. B. Dallery & C. E. Scott (Eds.), *The question of the other: Essays
    in contemporary continental philosophy* (pp. 35–43). New York: State Uni-
    versity of New York Press.
Cooper, K. & Hill, A. (2000). The language of school: Curricular goals and
    classroom life. *Teachers and Teaching: Theory and Practice, 6*(1), 63–73.
Daignault, J. (1992). Traces at work from different places. In W. F. Pinar &
    W. M. Reynolds (Eds.), *Understanding curriculum as phenomenological and
    deconstructed text* (pp. 195–215). New York: Teachers College Press.
Deleuze, G. (1993). *The Deleuze reader* (C. Boundas, Ed. and Trans.). New
    York: Columbia University Press.
Derrida, J. (1987). The ends of man. In K. Baynes, J. Bohman, & T. McCarthy
    (Eds.), *After Philosophy: End or Transformation* (pp. 119–158). Cambridge,
    MA: MIT Press.
Diffey, T. J. (1995). A note on some meanings of the term "aesthetic." *Journal
    of Aesthetics 35*(1), 61–63.
Eisner, E. (1992). Curriculum ideologies. In P. Jackson (Ed.), *Handbook of re-
    search on curriculum* (pp. 302–325). New York: Maxwell Macmillan.
Eliot, T. S. (1961). Burnt Norton. In M. Mack, L. Dean, & W. Frost (Eds.),
    Modern Poetry (2nd ed., pp. 169–175). Englewood Cliffs, NJ: Prentice Hall.
Elliott, J. (1991). *Action research for educational change.* Philadelphia: Open
    University Press.
Emerson, R. W. (1981). *The portable Emerson* (C. Bode, Ed.). New York: Vik-
    ing Press. (Original work published in 1946).
Estés, C. P. (1992). *Women who run with the wolves: Myths and stories of the
    wild woman archetype.* New York: Ballantine Books.

Farrell, J. (1996). From pinnacle to peon in twenty-five years. *Bell, Book & Candor.* Edmonton: Alberta Teachers' Association. (Original work published in 1971).

Fox, M. (1984). *Wilfred Gordon McDonald Partridge.* Toronto, ON: Puffin Books.

Gadamer, H. (1984). *Truth and method.* New York: Crossroad.

Gallagher, S. (1992). *Hermeneutics and education.* Albany: State University of New York Press.

Gerstein, M. (1986). *The seal mother.* New York: Dial Books for Young Readers.

Gilje, F. (1992). Being there: An analysis of the concept of presence. In D. Gauk (Ed.), *The presence of caring in nursing* (pp. 53–67). New York: National League for Nursing Press.

Grange, J. (1989). Lacan's other and the factions of Plato's soul. In A. B. Dallery & C. E. Scott (Eds.), *The question of the other: Essays in contemporary continental philosophy* (pp. 157–174). New York: State University of New York Press.

Greene, M. (1988). *The dialectic of freedom.* New York: Teachers College Press.

Greene, M. (2000). *Releasing the imagination: Essays on education, the arts, and social change.* San Francisco: Jossey-Bass.

Grumet, M. (1978). Songs and Situations: The figure ground relation in a case study of *Currere.* In G. Willis (Ed.), *Qualitative Evaluation* (pp. 276–315). Berkeley, CA: McCutchan.

Habermas, J. (1971). *Knowledge and human interests* (J. J. Shapiro, Trans.). Boston: Beacon Press.

Hegel, G. W. F. (1993). *Introductory lectures on aesthetics* (M. Inwood, Ed.; B. Bosanquet, Trans.). London: Penguin Books.

Heidegger, M. (1982). *On the way to language* (P. D. Hertz, Trans.). New York: Harper & Row.

Hill, A. (1994). Surprised by children: A call to pedagogical possibilities. *Canadian Journal of Education 19*(4), 339–350.

Hill, A., & Cooper, K. (1995). *Teachers' work: Pedagogical presence.* Paper presented at the Canadian Society for Studies in Education, University of Quebec at Montreal.

Hodgkin, R. A. (1985). *Playing and exploring: Education through the discovery of order.* London: Methuen.

Hoff, B. (1982). *The tao of Pooh.* New York: Viking Penguin Books.

Horowitz, M. (1995). *Career connections* (pp. 7–8). Edmonton: University of Alberta, Continuing Professional Education, Faculty of Education.

Johnson, M. (1989). Personal practical knowledge series: Embodied knowledge. *Curriculum Inquiry, 19*(4), 361–377.

Joyce, J. (1964). *A portrait of the artist as a young man.* Markham, ON: Penguin Books. (Original work published in 1916.)

Kristeva, J. (1981). *Le langage, cet inconnu* [Language, this unknown]. Paris: Editions du Seuil.

Langer, S. (1957). *Problems of art.* New York: Charles Scribner's Sons.

Langer, S. (1988). *Mind: An essay on human feeling.* London: Routledge & Kegan Paul.

Levin, D. M. (1985). *The body's recollection of being.* London: Routledge & Kegan Paul.

Levin, D. M. (1988). *The opening of vision.* London: Routledge.

Lippitz, W. (1986). Understanding children, communicating with children: Approaches to the child within us, before us, and with us. *Phenomenology + Pedagogy, 4*(2), 56–65.

Lovejoy, A. O. (1964). *The great chain of being: A study of the history of an idea.* Cambridge, MA: Harvard University Press. (Original work published in 1936)

Lyotard, J. (1984). *The postmodern condition: A report on knowledge.* (G. Bennington and B. Massumi, Trans.). Minneapolis: University of Minnesota Press.

MacNeil, R. (1988). Working Man. On *Reason to believe.* Lupin's Records/Virgin Music Canada. Audiocassette.

Marcuse, H. (1978). *The aesthetic dimension.* Boston: Beacon Press.

Merleau-Ponty, M. (1966). *Phenomenology of perception* (C. Smith, Trans.). New York: Routledge & Kegan Paul.

Merleau-Ponty, M. (1968). *The visible and the invisible* (C. Lefort, Ed.; A. Lingis, Trans.). Evanston, IL: Northwestern University Press.

Moore, L. (1989). *I'll meet you at the cucumbers.* New York: Bantam Skylark Book.

Nietzsche, F. (1969). *Thus spoke Zarathustra* (R. J. Hollingdale, Trans.). Markham, ON: Penguin Classics.

Olson, M. (1989). Room for learning. *Phenomenology + Pedagogy, 7,* 173–184.

O'Reilley, M. R. (1998). *Radical presence: Teaching as a contemplative practice.* Portsmouth, NH: Boynton/Cook.

Ovid. (1986). *Metamorphoses* (A. D. Melville, Trans.). Oxford: Oxford University Press.

Oxford English dictionary. (1933). Vol. 8. London: Oxford University Press.

Oxford English dictionary. (1964). Oxford: Clarendon Press.

Paille, P. (1994). Pour une methologogie de la complexite en education: le cas d'une recherche-action-formation [For a methodology of the complexity of education: the case of an research-action-formation]. *Canadian Journal of Education, 5,* 215–230.

Paley, V. (1986). On listening to what children say. *Harvard Educational Review, 56*(2), 122–131.

Paley, V. (1999). *The kindness of children.* Cambridge, MA: Harvard University Press.

Palmer, P. (1998). *The courage to teach.* New York: Jossey-Bass.

Pinar, W. (1988). "Whole, bright, deep with understanding": Issues in qualitative research and autobiographical method. In W. F. Pinar (Ed.), *Contemporary curriculum discourses* (pp. 134–153). Tuscon, AZ: Gorsuch Scarisbruck.

Polanyi, M. (1958). *Personal knowledge.* Chicago: Chicago University Press.

Polanyi, M. (1969). *Knowing and being.* London: Routledge & Kegan Paul.

Polanyi, M. (1983). *The tacit dimension.* Gloucester, MA: Peter Smith. (Original work published in 1966)

Polanyi, M., & Prosch, H. (1975). *Meaning.* Chicago: University of Chicago Press.

Proust, M. (1981). *Remembrance of things past: 3* (C. K. Moncrieff, T. Kilmartin, & A. Mayor, Trans.). London: Penguin Books.

Prigogine, I., & Stengers, I. (1984). *Order out of chaos: Man's new dialogue with nature.* New York: Bantam Books. (Original work published in 1979 under the title *La nouvelle alliance.*)

Ricard, F. (1994). Why the boomers never saved the world (D. Winkler, Trans.). *Saturday Night, 109*(8), 45–48.

Rich, A. (1978). *The dream of a common language.* New York: W. W. Norton.

Ricoeur, P. (1991). *From text to action: Essays in hermeneutics, II* (K. Blamey & J. B. Thompson, Trans.). Evanston, IL: Northwestern University Press.

Rilke, R. M. (1989). *The selected poetry of Rainer Maria Rilke* (S. Mitchell, Ed. and Trans.). New York: Vintage International.

Rosen, H. (1986). The importance of story. *Language Arts, 63*(3), 227–237.

Russell, T., & Munby, H. (1991). Reframing: The role of experience in developing teachers' professional knowledge. In D. A. Schon (Ed.), *The reflective turn* (pp. 164–187). New York: Teachers College Press.

Sallis, J. (1984). Heidegger/Derrida—Presence. *Journal of Philosophy, 81*(10), 594–610.

Sartre, J. (1956). *Being and nothingness*. New York: Philosophical Library.

Sartre, J. (1992). *Truth and existence* (A. van den Hoven, Trans.). Chicago: University of Chicago Press. (Original work established and annotated by A. Elkaim-Sartre)

Schon, D. (1987). *Educating the reflective practitioner*. San Francisco: Jossey-Bass.

Schon, D. (1991). Concluding comments. In D. A. Schon (Ed.), *The reflective turn: Case studies in and on educational practice* (pp. 343–359). New York: Teachers College Press.

Smith, D. (1991). Hermeneutic inquiry: The hermeneutic imagination and the pedagogic text. In E. Short (Ed.), *Forms of curriculum inquiry* (pp. 187–209). New York: State University of New York Press.

Smith, S. (1991). The security of the child's world. *Canadian Journal of Education, 16*(4), 442–452.

Smith, S. (1998). *Risk and our pedagogical relation to children: On the playground and beyond*. New York: State University of New York Press.

St. Exupéry, A. (1943). *The little prince* (K. Woods, Trans.). New York: Harcourt Brace Jovanovich.

Taylor, C. (1987). Overcoming epistemology. In K. Baynes, J. Bohman, & T. McCarthy (Eds.), *After philosophy: End or transformation* (pp. 459–488). Cambridge, MA: MIT Press.

Taylor, C. (1991). *The malaise of modernity*. Concord, ON: House of Anansi Press.

van Manen, M. (1986). *The tone of teaching*. Richmond Hill, ON: Scholastic.

van Manen, M. (1988). The relation between research and pedagogy. In W. F. Pinar (Ed.), *Contemporary curriculum discourses* (pp. 437–452). Tucson, AZ: Gorsuch Scarisbruck.

van Manen, M. (1991). *The tact of teaching: The meaning of pedagogical thoughtfulness*. London, ON: University of Western Ontario, Althouse Press.

Varela, F. J., Thompson, E. & Rosch, E. (1991). *The embodied mind: Cognitive and human experience*. Cambridge, MA: MIT Press.

Williams, M. (1983). *The velveteen rabbit*. New York: Holt, Reinhart and Wilson.

Wiseman, A. (1956). *The sacrifice*. Toronto: Macmillan.

Wittgenstein, L. (1953). *Philosophical investigations* (G. Anscombe, Ed.). Oxford: Basil Blackwell.

Witte, D., Sawada, D., & Hill, A. (1997). Dragon soup: Wittgenstein's language games in children's conversation and dramatic play, *Teaching Education, 9*(1).

Witte-Townsend, D., & Hill, A. (2005). Light-ness of being in the primary classroom: Inviting conversations of depth across educational communities, *Educational Theory and Philosophy* (in press).

Yeats, W. B. (1962). Among school children. In M. Abrams, E. Talbot Donaldson, R. Adams, S. Monk, G. Ford, & D. Daiches (Eds.), *The Norton anthology of English literature* (Vol. 2, pp. 1360–1362). New York: W. W. Norton. (Original work published in 1927.)

INDEX